uNforgettable

Your Roadmap to Being the Teacher They NEVER Forget

uNforgettable

Chuck Poole

The uN series

uNforgettable
© 2018 by Times 10 Publications

These books are available at special discounts when purchased in quantity for premiums, promotions, fundraising, and educational use. For inquiries and details, contact us at Times10Books.com.

Published by Times 10
Highland Heights, OH
Times10Books.com

Cover Design by Najdan Mancic
Interior Design by Steven Plummer
Editing by Carrie White-Parrish
Proofreading by Jennifer Jas

Library of Congress Cataloging-in-Publication Data is available.
ISBN: 978-1-948212-09-0
First Printing: September, 2018

Contents

uNveil a place to call home
uNravel a plan to make your classroom a home
uNleash the actions to show you care

uNveil the little things that matter
uNravel a way to connect with every student and show love
uNleash the investment

uNveil your light
uNravel a plan to shine through the storms and stay positive
uNleash kindness and give thanks

uNveil the true heroes
uNravel a plan to implement student voice and ownership
uNleash learning and break the mold

uNveil your struggles and successes
uNravel a plan to teach students to fail forward
uNleash failure without fear

uNveil true balance
uNravel a plan to have work-life balance
uNleash your newfound freedom

Dedication

To my wife, Amanda

This book is just as much yours as it is mine. You have been with me every step of the way and have inspired me to be better every day. You bring joy to every situation, and the lessons I have learned from you have made me a better person and a better teacher. Thank you for your unconditional love and your selfless patience with me through every adventure we take.

You are truly uNforgettable.

Preface

IT IS MY privilege and honor to partner with Times 10 Publications to produce The uNseries. Within every book in this series, we hope to reimagine teaching. Each author is a thought leader and difference-maker in education, and we are excited to bring their levels of genius to the books of The uNseries. We aim to provide tangible strategies and practical insights that will encourage, inspire, and empower teachers—so they can implement them right away. Ultimately, we hope to create a community of educators who can change the world. Together #WeTeachuN.

—CHUCK POOLE, PRODUCER OF THE UNSERIES AND
FOUNDER OF TEACHONOMY®

About The uNseries

Teaching Reimagined

THE GREATEST TEACHERS in the world are "uN." They are unlike the status quo. They are unforgettable, unstoppable, and unbreakable, and they carry out what others say is impossible. They are the ones who teach differently. As you read the books in The uNseries, my hope is that you begin to feel "uN" as well. In this series, we will embark on a road trip together and explore topics that are relevant and important to educators in entirely new ways. Each chapter will serve as a destination, a stop along the way, but will also exist separately from the other stops so that you can access the chapters as you like, rather than needing to read them chronologically. This is an adventure, and it should be one that you can make on your own. But just like any other road trip, this one will require a plan if you're to succeed. The destinations in each uNseries book are broken down into three stages to help you plan and navigate this map.

Three Stages of Your Road Trip

- **The uNveil.** This is the introductory part of the road trip—the planning aspect. The goal of this section is to unveil an important principle and introduce the chapter topic. We will focus on what to expect during the journey, as well as share inspiration to get you started.

- **The uNravel.** This is the GPS map that will help guide you through the plan. It lays out what you want to accomplish—and the directions for how to get there. The goal of this section is to set out specific guidelines for how to achieve what we discussed in the first section.

- **The uNleash.** This is the challenge you're going to set for yourself as you move forward. Here we're going to talk about the steps you can take right away to achieve the goals you've set for yourself, to build and then maintain your momentum toward becoming uNforgettable.

The uNseries is designed for educators, and I'll teach you how to use these steps to further your growth as a teacher, leader, and influencer. Together, we can become better than we ever could have alone—but only if we stick to our road-maps, which will give us the path to becoming uN. I am so excited to join you on this journey, and to see how you use uN to impact the world!

Introduction

A teacher's influence is one that never truly ends. It is an ever-present force that helps build character, strength, and wisdom for years to come. — CHUCK POOLE

Destination Guide Intro

Seventh Grade

MY TEACHING JOURNEY began when I was a scrawny seventh-grade student looking for acceptance. At that time, I had no idea that I would someday become a teacher. All I was worrying about was fitting in. During that year in middle school, however, I met an uNforgettable teacher who would change my life, and my path, forever.

Mr. William Bills was my physical education teacher and baseball coach. He not only taught me the curriculum with which he was provided, but also went above and beyond to teach me life lessons I still carry with me, and lessons that I teach my students today. He taught me about the importance of accepting others despite their differences, what it means to be a sponge when it comes to learning, and how a person's character is what earns true respect. After teaching me throughout high school, he continued to coach me in college, and we eventually began coaching side-by-side. We have continued doing so for over twenty years. He has had an indescribable impact on my life, as well as the lives of thousands of others, and all I can say to him is thank you for being uNforgettable.

His influence made me set a goal to become uN as well.

I have been blessed to have had *many* teachers whom I will never forget. They each have had a hand in molding me into the teacher I am today, and because of their impact, I am driven to continue in their footsteps and influence the next generation.

About uNforgettable

My desire is to encourage and inspire teachers everywhere to impact and influence their students, much like Mr. Bills did for me. I sincerely hope that every teacher becomes someone's "uNforgettable." My inspiration and ideas shared throughout this book come from my own experiences, the experiences of my students, and the numerous uNforgettable teachers from whom I had the privilege to learn. Every student deserves a teacher he or she will never forget, and throughout *uNforgettable*, I focus on the intangibles that give teachers spark. This book is not about ignoring curriculum or forgetting what great teaching looks like, because those components are crucial if we're going to make a complete impact. Rather, it is about enhancing our teaching and the experiences we offer to our students, intertwining intangible strategies like creating community and encouraging ownership, and finding the balance in it all. Most of all, this book is about recognizing and building relationships—because the relationships we have with our students, our colleagues, our content, and ourselves are what make us uNforgettable.

Who Is This Book For?

This book is for the trailblazers who want to make a real difference in the lives of the students they teach. It is for those who inspire kids to be remarkable and help them believe that they can achieve their dreams. It is for those who love the unlovable, accept the unacceptable, rebuild the broken, and help the geniuses soar. This book is for teachers who are on a journey toward making this world a better place. If you believe in your students, refer to them as "my kids," or have a contagious passion for making sure they have a better future, then this book is for you.

In *uNforgettable,* there are ten destinations for teachers to explore that will help them truly impact their students. Reaching these destinations will help you to stick in the hearts and minds of your students forever. As we travel through this book, my hope is that you find inspiration and encouragement to change the world one student at a time.

For this particular book, I will be your guide on the journey. At the beginning of each chapter, you'll find a QR Code that will send you to a short video and a reflection guide associated with that chapter. If you'd prefer to access the material via your computer, find it at **unseries.com/reflectionguide**. In these videos, I personally walk you through what to expect from the chapter and touch on the importance of the topic at hand. The reflection guide will give you the opportunity to delve deeper into what you have discovered and cement it into your practice right away. My goal is to be by your side for the entire journey. I don't have all the answers, but I know that by the time we reach the last chapter, we will both be a little closer to impacting the world in an even greater way than we could have imagined when we began.

I can't wait to go on this journey with you!

Create a Home

The ache for home lives in all of us. The safe place where we can go as we are and not be questioned. — MAYA ANGELOU

Destination Guide One
••••••••••••••••••••••••••••••••

WHEN THEY CAN'T WAIT TO
TELL YOU ABOUT A BIG EVENT
IN THEIR LIVES, OR THEY
RANDOMLY HIGH-FIVE OR
HUG YOU FOR NO REASON,
IT MEANS THEY ARE HOME.

uNveil a Place to Call Home

WELCOME HOME.

No matter how much we travel or how often we go away, there is always one place we look forward to getting back to: home. It is the place where we feel most comfortable, loved, and free. Home is where we are accepted for who we are by those we love the most. After a long day at work, home is where we go to put our feet up and relax or spend much-needed time with family. It is where we share stories that are sometimes filled with laughter and other times filled with tears. It is the one place where most of us can go, and regardless of what has happened in our lives, we will always feel welcomed.

As teachers, if we provide a place for our students that *feels* like that idea of home, we can change the way they view learning. Imagine if your classroom was a place your students looked forward to going to every day–a place where they felt welcomed, regardless of what the outside world was doing at that moment. How much would that change their feelings about walking into your space? When the door to your classroom opens, you have the chance to offer hope, security, and acceptance to students who may not be experiencing it anywhere else. We get to mold minds, influence the future leaders of our world, and impact individuals every day. There is no better place to do that than a place that feels like home.

Even better, if we create a home for our students, we also create something that will extend *beyond* our classroom walls. When students see a teacher they love outside of school and they grow wide-eyed with excitement and start to grin with anticipation, it means they are home. When they can't wait to tell you about a big event in their lives, or they randomly high-five or hug you for no reason, it means they are home. An uNforgettable teacher is a teacher who makes a student feel loved and cared for—like family. An uNforgettable teacher becomes like a piece of home for those students, and the classroom becomes a safe haven. Creating this type of environment for our students is a gift that they will cherish for their entire lives, and it is a gift that each one of them deserves.

So how do we do that? The easiest way to start on this journey is to take a deeper look at what a home is, and then make our classrooms match it. We can become uNforgettable teachers when we replicate home life and create a place where students *want* to be. These teachers maintain a welcoming, accepting, family environment.

A Home Provides Family

The story of *The Wizard of Oz* is a great example of the power of family and its connection to home. When Dorothy is in Oz, she meets three main companions: the scarecrow, the tin man, and the cowardly lion. Each one is a representation of a family member she misses in Kansas. Although she is admired, rewarded, and even hailed as a hero in Oz, Dorothy only feels at home when she is with those who love her for who she truly is. She goes to a completely different land—but finds her family there, and sticks with them.

And teachers can learn from that. No, we don't need a classroom that resembles Oz to follow this example. We simply need a loving heart that accepts our students as they are. We need to give them a place where they feel like they belong, become their family, and create an environment in which they feel as though the students around them are family. Years from now, students won't remember the decorations in the classroom, the rewards they received, or the gadgets we used to impress them. Rather, they will remember the listening ear of the teacher who stood by their sides in a time of need. They will remember the pride they felt when they were told they did a great job. They will remember the teachers they accidentally called "Mom" or "Dad," because to them those teachers were family. When our classroom feels like home, our students feel loved—and that love is a connection they will never forget.

This must extend toward the entire classroom because a family is built when people with different personalities and backgrounds come together and bond. An uNforgettable teacher is one who can blend together different students in a way that helps them form a family. Many of us do this every day. When we teach our students to embrace their differences, we encourage acceptance, and when we share a moment with them in a time of need, we build trust. A family is built on trust and acceptance, and when we take the time to nourish these two things, we offer our students a much-needed element of what a loving home provides: safety.

A Home Provides Safety

A home must go beyond feeling familiar and family oriented. It must also feel secure. When we find a place where we can be ourselves, we feel safe. Many of our students face unimaginable experiences outside of our classrooms and have no place to take refuge. Even their homes may be off balance and insecure. Others live pretty normal lives and have plenty of places to call home. We can provide a place where each one of them, regardless of their circumstances, will feel *safe*. They need a place they can run to when they are stressed or overwhelmed, where they won't have to worry about failing. If we build classroom environments that include safety nets waiting to catch those students if they fall, they will feel safe and secure in those classrooms. That safety will grow to include trust, and with that trust comes an uNforgettable bond.

uNravel a Plan to Make Your Classroom a Home

If we want to be uNforgettable teachers, we need to make our students feel that sort of home-like comfort and belonging in our classrooms. We need to offer them a space where they look forward to going to each day—a place where they feel welcome, like how a guest should feel at a friend's house. When our students wait for our classroom doors to open each day, they should feel like a guest waiting on the welcome mat of your home, antici-pating a positive greeting followed by a wonderful visit.

The first thing people see when they enter most homes is that welcome mat. Some friends will dust their feet off on it while others will look down and simply read what it says, but they all notice it. It serves as a comforting starting point because once they pass that mat, we greet them with a smile, a handshake, or a hug, and the visit begins. When things start with a warm introduction and something familiar, people feel at home.

Our students deserve that same treatment—to be welcomed into the classroom like honored guests—and uNforgettable teachers do their best to make sure it happens every day.

The reality, of course, is that the day-to-day business of teaching can often cause us to overlook these simple ges-tures. We can become so caught up in what we need to get done or what we have to teach that we forget to slow down and take in the moment. We forget to make our students wel-come guests in our class-rooms. The key is to remember that it doesn't take a lot of time to change it and to make your stu-dents feel at home. Our largest impact is in the

THE MONTHLY MINGLE IS ONE STRATEGY FOR TURNING A SHORT PERIOD OF TIME INTO AN EXPERIENCE THAT HELPS STUDENTS FEEL LIKE FAMILY, AND A CLASSROOM FEEL LIKE HOME.

25

smallest moments, and in the end, we can teach them more when we take the time to love first and teach second.

Treat your students like they are valuable, and show them that you are genuinely interested in who they are, and you will impact their learning on a totally different level. One simple way to begin this process is to take a moment to mingle with your students and provide something like a family get-together. The Monthly Mingle is one strategy for turning a short period of time into an experience that helps students feel like family, and a classroom feel like home.

The Monthly Mingle

Our students want attention. Some of them spend all day trying to impress us, while others drive us crazy to get noticed. Some will shy away, hoping that we will see them and ask about their day, because nobody else in their lives ever does. Regardless of how they demonstrate it, these students are looking for someone to prove to them that they matter. To make them feel like family. And those students will never forget a teacher who goes out of the way to do exactly that.

The beauty of family get-togethers is that they provide an opportunity for connecting with other people. We have a chance to catch up with one another, ask questions, and share. When we are with our families, we make sure to give everyone we encounter a little time and attention. The Monthly Mingle strategy takes that concept into the classroom each month, with the goal of giving students the chance to feel like family "catching up" with each other, and with you as their teacher.

How It Works

1. Schedule a Monthly Mingle (or a Weekly Mingle, if you prefer) at the end of each month or week. Set aside approximately ten minutes for the mingling session.

2. Prepare three simple, open-ended questions in advance. For example, share questions like, "If you could change one thing in your life, what would it be and why?" or "What is one thing that has happened this week that made you smile?" or a question as simple as, "What is something that makes you happy?"

3. Present the first question, then set the students loose and allow them to mingle with each other and discuss the question.

4. Provide two rules:

   • Rule One: Stand up (if they're able to) and move around the classroom to mingle.

   • Rule Two: Discuss each question with two or more people.

5. Join them in mingling, and start with the shy or reserved students. The key is to get them talking about themselves.

6. Write down the things that stand out to you during your conversations.

7. Repeat these steps with the other two questions.

8. At the end of the session, bring the class together for a "family minute" and share one thing you appreciate about the group.

9. Follow up. Make sure to follow up with students over the next few days on points that you wrote down during the conversations. When they realize that you were truly listening, they will feel important—and you will get closer to becoming an uNforgettable teacher in their lives.

Embrace the Power of Personal Touch

Our homes are filled with personal memories on display for all to see. Whether they are pictures of loved ones or mementos from places we've been, we are proud to let others catch a glimpse of our lives through them. It is a combination of what we display and what we personally share that turns our house into a home, and causes others to come back to visit time and time again.

When we take that into the classroom and add our own personal touches to our spaces, the same thing happens, and our students feel more connected to us. They start to realize we are real people with lives outside of teaching, and that contrary to what they tend to believe, we don't live in the school. The atmosphere we create invites our students to spend a little time inside our worlds. It allows them a glimpse into our interests and passions, and inspires them to share theirs as well. This also adds to the safety of the space and increases the feeling of family.

The simple, personal touches we put into our classrooms are what students will remember forever. uNforgettable teachers are willing to make themselves vulnerable and transparent in order to inspire their students. They're willing to allow students into their lives—and they're also willing to venture into their students' lives. By displaying our lives and sharing who we are, we build the foundation toward becoming uNforgettable.

Three Simple Personal Touches

The question remains: What should we add to our personal spaces—and what might constitute overstepping our boundaries? This is, after all, a delicate line, and we must tread carefully as we allow students further into our personal lives. Use the following guidelines as a map:

Personal Touch One:
What you display

Place pictures of family, friends, and loved ones in view for students to see. This simple personal touch gives your students insight into who you are and what you value. It makes them feel as if they know you a little bit better, and that gives them the idea that they can also talk to you about life and what matters most to them. Display examples of your own interests—as well as work from your students—on your walls, and pull them together into themed sections. Favorite movie posters, quotes, or sports memorabilia will bring up conversations and inspire students to ask questions and get to know you better. And the better they get to know you, the more comfortable they'll start to feel with you, and the more like family you'll become. When we display the people and interests that we hold most dear, we create an atmosphere that feels like home to anyone who steps inside.

Personal Touch Two:
What you share

Make it a point to share personal stories about your life whenever they relate to the concepts you are teaching. They can be funny or sentimental, but should always give you a chance to be transparent and real. You'll be surprised by how your students respond. When we lead by example and share pieces of ourselves, our students will follow.

Though your stories should usually be spontaneous, try to plan at least one personal story a week as an example, motivation, or segue. When we plan them in, we are guaranteed to share them. You'll be amazed at how sharing personal stories becomes contagious—and makes the classroom feel more like a family home.

Personal Touch Three:
What you do

The things that make us different also make us memorable, so embrace your unique teaching—and living—styles. Some teachers are funny, while others are dry. Some are laid back while others are extremely strict. Your style is what gives your students variety. uNforgettable teachers find the best strategies for helping their students learn, and then present them in a way that is consistent with who they are. Be proud of who you are and maintain your own personal style when you teach. What you do and how you do it leaves a great impact, and when you are comfortable in your own skin, the students in your classroom will feel more at home in theirs.

Show Them, Don't Tell Them

A family doesn't necessarily need to tell each other how they feel, because the love they share is evident through their actions. Although words can be reassuring, our actions have to back them up—and it's those actions that leave a lasting impression. We often impact our students more with what we don't say than with what actually comes out of our mouths, and in many cases, our students will remember our actions and responses even more than our words. When students experience a teacher's love, it will change them forever. Show your students you care by being present in their lives when they need you, following through on what you say, and demonstrating kindness to them. Those actions will welcome them home every day, and continue to make the classroom a safe space—and their teacher someone they can count on.

Show Up, Follow Through, Be Kind

Creating a comforting atmosphere and adding personal touches are both key elements in building a home for your students because they open the door to a foundational element found in any place we call home: a personal connection. Give them that, and the memories they make in your classrooms will last in their hearts forever and will guarantee you a place in their stories. Adopt the following three actions as guidelines to help create that personal connection that so many students need in their lives:

- **Show up.** Our students do so much outside of our classrooms. They might compete in sports, participate in the school play, or play an instrument in the band. And most of the time, the only people who watch them do these activities are their immediate families. One thing that lights up students' faces like nothing else is when a teacher shows up to watch them do something other than sit in class. Find out about your students' talents, and make it a point to show up when they get to demonstrate them. Sometimes all students need in order to feel like family is for a teacher to show up and support them.

- **Follow through.** Our students want to be heard. When they make suggestions, show them that you are listening by following through and carrying those suggestions out, or at least responding to them with variations of your own.

When they tell you that something important is going on in their lives, follow up with them after a few days to find out how it went. Doing this can make all the difference when it comes to making students feel special. When we follow through with our students, we show them that we care. When they know that we view them as valuable individuals, they start to feel as if they truly matter to us—and that increases their confidence in the classroom. Follow through and follow up with your students as often as possible, and make sure you're demonstrating an interest in something other than academics, to become truly uNforgettable.

- **Be kind.** We tell our students to be kind all the time, and though we might do our best to be a model of that in every situation, it can be hard. If you want to create a home for your students, make sure that kindness is your first response in any situation. When students enter your classroom, give them random compliments as they take their seats. Make it a point to give them small notes of encouragement throughout the week to let them know you are proud of them, or call home to tell parents about things their children are doing well. Simple acts of kindness will cause students to want to be around you, and will help them feel at home in your classroom.

uNleash the Actions to Show You Care

Now that we have covered the importance of making students feel at home in our classrooms, and learned a few ways to make the classroom more homelike, it's time to pull it all together into one week's worth of easy activities. Building a home is a process that happens one building block at a time. A home should be a safe place of acceptance and comfort, but as we know, not all students experience this in their lives outside of school. We have the opportunity to provide such an environment, and showing your students that you care can give them something they'll never forget. Getting to know their interests, showing up at their extracurricular activities, and simply letting them catch a glimpse of who you are so that they feel welcome can make all the difference in their lives. Creating a home will take patience and dedication, but the end result is truly remarkable. Follow it up with action to become truly uNforgettable. Follow these three steps to cement this into your weekly—and everyday—schedule:

- **Reflect.** Start your journey forward by reflecting on what you do now and how you can improve, in light of the information in the prior sections. Think about your current classroom environment. What personal touches or comforting elements do you display that help make your students feel safe? When it comes to your relationships with your students, how do your day-to-day interactions help them feel at home? How can you improve on those? What can you do to make the space feel even more welcoming?

- **uNleash.** After you've adjusted the space inside your classroom, take the next steps toward making your classroom a family—starting with yourself. Tell a story. Plan a mingle. Show up. This is where you take the crucial step of moving from reflecting on what you have learned to actually putting it into action. A thought without action is simply a dream that will never come true. Choose one of these three actions and uNleash a plan to make it happen this week.

  - Think of one personal story that you can tell this week to engage your students in a lesson.

  - Plan a Monthly Mingle and put it on your schedule. Write three simple questions you will use during the mingle.

  - Plan to show up to something that your students are involved in that takes place outside your classroom. It will impact them more than you realize.

- **Get social:** Take a photo of your classroom or share what you've done to make your classroom a home for your students. Post it on social media using the hashtag #WeTeachuN to inspire other teachers and give them ideas for what they can do in their own classrooms to create a family environment.

Love Every Student

Every kid is one caring adult away from being a success story. — JOSH SHIPP

Destination Guide Two

WE NEVER KNOW WHICH
ACTION WILL BE THE PEBBLE
THAT BEGINS THE RIPPLE,
BUT EACH PEBBLE IS WORTH
THROWING BECAUSE
SOMETIMES ALL IT TAKES
IS ONE LITTLE ACTION TO
CHANGE THE LANDSCAPE
OF A STUDENT'S LIFE.

uNveil the Little Things That Matter

THERE IS POWER in a pebble.

When a lake is still on a calm day, it almost looks like a mirror. The surrounding landscape is reflected on its surface, and time itself feels like it has momentarily stopped. The pebbles that rest on the bank of the lake may seem insignificant in comparison to that overwhelming scenery in front of them ... but there is power in a pebble. One tiny pebble, when dropped in that still lake, will cause a ripple that will break the stillness and spread throughout the entire width and length of the lake itself. What once seemed small and insignificant will change the horizon with its impact, and turn a still lake into one that is filled with movement and vigor.

Our students are a lot like a still lake. Some reflect and reveal the best qualities of those around them, while others do their best to remain motionless despite our best efforts to reach them. But if our students are like a lake, then we are the pebbles that might affect them. Regardless of which side of the spectrum they fit into, and even if they are somewhere in between, every student we teach will benefit from the pebbles we drop into their lives. Luckily, uNforgettable teachers are filled with pebbles. With each piece of encouragement you give, every lesson you teach, and the tough love you demonstrate from time to time, your influence grows. The ripple effect of the pebbles you drop will not soon be forgotten, and what may seem insignificant in the moment will impact students in ways you may never even realize.

When students are caring, kind, and responsible, it is a pleasure to have them in class. When they are disruptive, disrespectful, and irresponsible, however, it can be a totally different story. Our goal is to love all students, regardless of their circumstances, because through that love we can build relationships and impact those we teach. We demonstrate that love in the little things we do each day. From time to time, we might have students who test our patience, and we may say or do something we regret later. A small apology to that student, and admitting we were wrong, is a pebble that will begin a ripple. When a student has a talent that no one else praises, a simple compliment will bring about a smile. When we are persistent in showing we care, even when students act like they don't need it, we drop a pebble.

We never know which action will be the pebble that begins the ripple, but each pebble is worth throwing because sometimes all it takes is one little action to change the landscape of a student's life. Our students will benefit from our knowledge and will appreciate our help, but they will never forget a teacher who showed them they were important and made them feel loved.

Loving Every Student Requires Patience

When we love others, we are willing to be patient with them when they frustrate us, because our relationship with them is more important than any angry outburst in the moment. Although the issue at hand may be important, we concentrate more on the persons in front of us, because our reaction to them is based on more than simply winning an argument. To love all students, you must maintain your awareness of how you react to them, especially during times of frustration. Love requires patience, so maintain your ability to wait calmly in the face of frustration. At times, you will come across a student who seems impossible to handle—and your patience will make an impact all on its own. Although it will not be easy, practicing patience in the small moments will demonstrate your love over time. This pebble is a lack of reaction rather than an action—but that does not make it any less uNforgettable.

When you feel like your patience is being tested, take a minute to pause and reflect before you respond. For example, if a student says something disrespectful during class, instead of lashing out or responding in frustration, pause and address the comment directly. Pull the student aside afterward and explain why the comment was wrong and how he or she can fix it moving forward. The student will understand, consciously or subconsciously, that you're responding with love and teaching how to handle similar situations. Take the time to follow this model whenever this situation occurs, and you'll learn to put your students before your emotions.

Our initial reaction to confrontation is often to say the first thing that comes to mind, without thinking. Instead, practice patience during these times by simply pausing, reflecting, and then responding. Before you react, take a moment and breathe, reflect on how the student in front of you needs you more than you may realize, and then respond in a way that will bring about a positive outcome or teach a lesson. Depending on the situation, you may need to encourage them—or you may need to show them a bit of firm discipline. Either way, the key is to lead with love by practicing patience and taking a moment to think before you react.

When students are disrespectful or test our patience, they are usually doing so in an attempt to get attention. Consider that they might be looking for attention because they have issues somewhere else in their lives. It might be that something is going on at home, or that something frustrating happened during their day. And although some students will require more patience than others, all students deserve to feel as if they have an outlet for their needs. Give them that support, show them a patient love that many of them have never experienced before, and you will become the teacher that they find uNforgettable.

Loving Every Student Requires Hope

Patience is important, but hope is nearly as beneficial to our students' mental well-being. Hope is not wishful thinking, but rather the expectation that a certain thing is going to happen. Every student you teach deserves to expect success, and you can demonstrate your love for them by teaching them how to cultivate hope—which many of them have never experienced. Show students that you expect great things from them and you will begin to instill belief, and in turn, spark hope.

Teach your students to hope, and you will become the person who sits at the foundation of their goals and aspirations. They will look to you as their guide because their hope will be rooted in the love you showed by believing in them. This goes beyond teaching them the approved curriculum and allows you to invest in them as the amazing people they are.

MANY STUDENTS WILL GIVE UP WHEN THEY HIT A ROADBLOCK, BUT YOU'RE IN A POSITION TO DEMONSTRATE THAT THERE MIGHT BE SEVERAL DIFFERENT STRATEGIES FOR ACHIEVING EACH GOAL.

People who have hope know how to do three things well. They can set goals, find different pathways to achieve those goals, and demonstrate the grit needed to stick with their goals when things get tough. We have the unique opportunity to instill these three things into each student. Start by teaching them that failure to meet a goal is not an end, but rather a detour that leads to a different path, and you will show them hope. Many students will give up when they hit a roadblock, but you're in a position to demonstrate that there might be several different strategies for achieving each goal. Give them direction, and help them approach their goals, no matter how big or small, with action. Teach them how to set and accomplish goals, and it will serve them well for years to come. Use the following five steps to help them kick-start their goals right from the beginning and teach them what it feels like to hope:

1. Create a "why" list where they record their purpose or motivation behind achieving the goal.

2. Tell people about what they are setting out to do. This accountability step is crucial when it comes to accomplishing goals.

3. Break up the larger goal into smaller, more achievable steps. This makes the goal more manageable and gives them smaller successes along the way.

4. Set a date for the end of the journey to establish a specific timeline.

5. Create reward check-ins, and give themselves small rewards when they accomplish steps along the way. This makes larger goals more manageable and helps them maintain motivation and optimism during the process.

Love every student you teach by adding your own hope to their process. When they see you cheering them on, standing in their corner and expecting them to succeed at the goals they set for themselves, they will see hope in action. Students are searching for someone to show them that they can succeed and give them the confidence they need to accomplish their dreams. An uNforgettable teacher fills that position by caring deeply for students, focusing on their limitless potential, and offering them the hope they need to keep working at something until they find success.

uNravel a Way to Connect with Every Student and Show Love

Every student we teach is different, and our relationships with them determine how we show them the love we've been talking about. Whether we are building trust and respect through our patience or teaching them to hope through goal setting, we must show them constantly that they are loved. You'll build close relationships with some of your students, while others will keep their distance, but your goal with all students is to show you care about them. To do this, consider not only your relationships with the students but also their individual learning and personal needs.

Make a "Relationship Investment"

Treat your relationships with your students as lifetime investments, and make sure you're adjusting those investments to fit the students themselves. Believe in the bright future awaiting each student, and figure out how you can help them get there. Start investing on the first day of the year to build the foundation for strong, trusting relationships later in the year, and keep in mind that it won't happen overnight. Just like in life, investments take time, and your investments in your student will travel over hills and through valleys before you see them grow to fruition.

Maintain your patience, though, and don't let the timeline throw you off the investment.

When it comes to investing, experts often recommend getting into the market when it's at its lowest. For example, when we look to invest in the stock market, we try to invest when the stock is low, rather than high, because our return will be much greater. When we are purchasing a home, we want to do it when interest rates and housing prices are as low as possible, so our money will go further. Use the same rule when it comes to your relationships with students. They need us—and our hope and support—when they are at their lowest. Difficult, unruly, and disrespectful students might be at their low points and need someone to pay attention and reach out to save them.

Doing so at that moment guarantees that you are investing in them when they're at their lowest points, and teachers who do so become uNforgettable. A truly uNforgettable teacher invests in students during their struggles, as well as during their successes. When we show them that we care even during tough times, we show them that they're more than just a student in a classroom.

Try one of the following investment strategies with your students as you continue to build relationships with them. Some may work well with certain students, while some may not. Be discerning in every case, and take the time to invest wisely. These investment strategies can serve as a starting point as you venture into their lives.

The Silent Investment

Relationships grow through encouragement, and the most powerful connections are sometimes those of silence. We all know someone who has made us feel good about ourselves. When an administrator gives us a look of approval, followed by a smile, to tell us that they noticed our hard work, we feel like we can conquer the world. When parents send an email to thank us for being a positive influence in the life of their child, and tell us that we are the subject at dinner on many nights, it makes us glow with pride. It is often the silent, small gestures that only we see that make the most impact because we are being recognized. Every student deserves to have that from time to time because that feeling is love put into action.

One way to give them their own personal standing ovation is through a silent investment: a simple note of encouragement for a job well done. When students have done something well or are feeling low, handwrite notes that praise them for who they are and what they bring to the class. This will show them that you are proud of them and will serve as a building block for a trusting relationship. Do not make a big deal of it; instead, simply hand it to them or slip it into their notebook. The individualized attention will make it more personal, and to many, that will be even more special.

Save these silent investments for when students need them most, and make sure you're not overusing them. Keep them special so that you don't dilute their impact.

The Public Investment

Although some students may not seek public praise, others are looking for it. Some people love to be recognized in the public eye. If your students are old enough, they'll no doubt be active on social media and concerned with things like followers, likes, and subscribers. Those are the students who need public approval, which boosts their confidence and makes them feel loved.

Use the public investment for those students to give them the biggest possible boost. Remember that this shouldn't be a reward for doing something well, but rather a celebration of the students themselves. Plan something like a ceremony each month, or some sort of weekly recognition process. Take time out of class and tell the students—publicly—what you think of them and why you're proud of the progress they're making. Do this in front of their peers to validate them and begin to form a connection that they will always remember.

The Scheduled Investment

Whether you are investing in your students privately or publicly, remember that *every* student deserves your attention. Forgetting a student makes the student feel as if he or she is unloved. Teachers' lives are busy, and we can sometimes overlook things. At times, a student might begin telling you a story on a busy morning, and you might dismiss the student without listening. Unless you ask the student about it again later in the day, he or she will feel forgotten—and you'll lose a chance to connect. In doing so, you might lose the connection with this student for an entire year. So how do you avoid incidents like that? You *schedule* your investments.

The scheduled investment works best with a group of students, but it can work with one as well. The key is to plan it into your daily schedule. Start by setting aside one day each week when you sacrifice a little time to invest in your students. Find something that a group of students is interested in and create a themed meeting around it. Invite them to have lunch with you so you can share in their interests. Create an extension activity that connects to something you taught in class that students demonstrated an interest in, and offer to meet with them to explore more. Doing so allows you to connect an outside activity with learning—and connect with the students themselves. Treat this investment like an appointment you cannot miss and put it into your calendar ahead of time. Spend the date focusing on their needs, and come prepared to talk about their interests and what they need help with in order to improve in school. The goal of the scheduled investment is to show your students they are important enough for individualized attention outside of the normal class time. When your attention is focused on what they are interested in, you'll start to build a foundation of trust and long-term support.

Never Give Up on Them

Once you have invested in your students, they will come to expect consistency. They will rely on you to be the one they can count on through the year. If there is one thing students love to do, however, it is to test their teachers. When they put your love for them to the test, consider this a challenge that you cannot fail. Many of your students have experienced situations in which adults gave up on them at the first sign of trouble, but an uNforgettable teacher will never give up on students.

You must *refuse* to give up on them, no matter what they throw at you.

When they realize that you are going to stick with them no matter what, it can transform their mindsets and maximize your impact. Take that one step further and commit to keeping them accountable to their goals, and you'll show them that you're not going to allow them to quit on themselves, either. When they see that you're keeping them accountable because you have ultimate faith in them, your connection with them will solidify.

So what exactly do you keep students accountable for, and how do you do it in a way that shows love and patience? Keeping track of every student's progress in all aspects of school can be difficult, and in some ways, impossible. Simplify the process by choosing one or two specific areas for each student. One way to do this is by having students create goal cards, and helping them track their progress along the way. With goal cards, you become part of the process and an important support system for them as they work on their achievements—and you are able to get involved with each student in your class, without fail.

Student Goal Cards

Some of the most successful people in the world write down their goals. They do so because people are more successful in what they set out to do when they write down a plan and refer to it often. Many of our students have goals they would like to achieve, and may even refer to them during a conversation, but if they do not take a moment to write them down, they may simply forget about them.

Student Goal Cards are simple 4-by-6-inch note cards where students write two specific goals. Punch a hole in the cards so that students can attach them to a three-ring binder, keychain, or anything they carry with them every day. On the card itself, direct them to write one personal goal they would like to achieve (and make sure it has nothing to do with school)—and one learning goal (that has nothing to do with grades). Then have them break their goals into actionable steps that will lead to successful outcomes. Each actionable step should be a small part of the entire goal. For example, if a student has the goal of creating an app, the student will be far more successful if he or she understands the steps that go along with it. Step one could be to decide on the purpose of the app, and step two could be to decide on which programming language to use. Step three could be to learn the basics of the programming language, and so on.

Our job is to guide them as they go, and to celebrate each step that they complete. Treat each successful step as an accomplishment that gets them closer to achieving what they set out to do, and help them check off those steps on their cards. Provide your own time to give them support when things go wrong, and prove to them that you're going to be with them at every point—without giving up on them. Make yourself someone they can depend on and they will never forget you.

We all tell our students that we will never give up on them. It doesn't become believable, however, until we follow through and take action to show them we mean it. Take the time to walk through the goal-setting process with them and you will demonstrate your belief that they can achieve great things, and your commitment to staying with them to the end.

The key to success with student goal setting is accountability and follow through. We need to set the example and then provide them with opportunities to "check in" often, in order to track their progress. With our busy schedules, it can be difficult to keep up with every student, but the following strategies will help you simplify the process and make all students feel valuable while they are on their journeys to success.

Easy Ways to Check In and Help Students Track Their Progress

1. Encourage students to partner up with classmates who will keep them accountable. You may need to assign them, in some cases. Once a week, conduct a quick, five-minute check-in where students discuss their progress with their partners and share ideas that can help them move forward.

2. Conduct a random "handshake and hint." When students are settling in, choose one or two each day and simply give them a handshake (or a high-five) and ask to see their goal cards. Ask about their progress. Once they tell you, share with them a hint or two on how they can continue moving forward to meet their goals.

3. Plan Mentor Moments. We teach our students life lessons just about every day. A Mentor Moment is when we get even more specific and cater the life lessons we teach to the goals they have set. Plan to talk to a few students each week and give them extra wisdom and encouragement as they go about their day. Ask to see their goal cards a few days in advance and make notes about their goals. When you meet with them, give them extra insight into how you have seen them grow in the specific areas you noted as you read their cards. This simple moment may seem random to them, but the encouragement and advice will help them soar—and planning it in advance will give you time to prepare exactly what to say.

Develop Connection Points

Students will appreciate the increased attention, but they also want to be accepted by their peers. One way to love all students is to make sure they are well connected to those around them. Unfortunately, many of our students slip through the cracks and get lost in the shuffle of school. We must make sure that each of them feels loved, not only by us but also by their peers. This can be difficult and daunting, but the key is to look for patterns in student interactions and their behaviors toward one another throughout the school day. Look for how they treat each other in your class, as well as in any other setting. Once we've found those locations, we can use our influence to help them develop connections. Our students look to us to be the ones who guide them through their day, and our influence with them goes far beyond the content we teach. They tell us personal stories, share heartwarming memories, and rely on us to lift them up when they are down, simply because they care about what we think of them. This type of influence is powerful, and when we use it to help them connect with one another, we can change their world.

A Simple Way to Help Students Connect and Create Bonds

Students love choice, and they love to sit or work with their friends as much as possible. When we let them choose who they want to work with, however, one or two students will probably linger awkwardly and eventually have to be assigned a group or a seat. Doing this does more harm than good because we are acknowledging that those students don't have anyone they want to sit with, which damages their self-esteem. In many cases, the students who were not chosen feel unwanted, and we unintentionally reinforce their belief that they do not matter. We can love our students and do everything in our power to make them feel accepted, but if their peers do not welcome them, it will be difficult to convince them of anything different.

We do have control when it comes to what students do in our classrooms, though, and although we cannot force students to like each other, we can make a difference. Try managing the seating process to create a clique-free environment in class. Make it a point to mix up the seating often, and set the precedent that seating choice is an opportunity to expand friendships and to alter the classroom culture. The goal is to create a safe space where all students work together, regardless of who they choose.

So how can we allow students to choose their seats *and* eliminate the constant isolation that some students feel? This is not an easy task, yet if we find a way to connect our students with one another consistently, friendships will form and isolation can disappear. Try the following three-step process to solve this problem:

Step One: Allow students to choose who they would like to work with every other week. Simply ask them to put their name and their partner's name on a notecard and hand it in for consideration. Then start a schedule. During the first week, you get to choose who they work with. During the second, they get to choose for themselves. And so on.

Step Two: Review choices and keep track of patterns. Take note of who is constantly left out, or who hands in a notecard with no partner written down at all. These are the students you need to pay special attention to because they're the ones who need help bonding with their peers. Set up a time to talk with the isolated students, as well as students who are well connected, and get to know their interests. Then make decisions and bring some of them

together based on what you've seen. You can create terrific new friendships, and the fact that you've taken the time to do this will make you uNforgettable to all the students involved.

Step Three: On student choice weeks, allow students to sit with their choices, and place the isolated students (those with no partner chosen) with those who would fit them best according to their interests. Since the groups are made based on the cards you received, the students that have not been chosen will not be isolated publicly. On teacher choice weeks, you might also try placing students together based on their strengths and commonalities. Mix them up a bit and give them an opportunity to sit with different people each week.

The goal of this activity is not to simply mix seating options, but to help students bond with those who they may not have chosen on their own. It also provides a comfortable way for shy and withdrawn students to meet classmates and make long-lasting friends. Some of our most isolated students dream of having friends, and if we want to love and connect with every student we teach, we have to provide opportunities for them to respect and love each other as well.

uNleash the Investment

When students feel loved by a teacher, they have the confidence to exceed expectations and soar to heights they never thought possible. Sometimes it only takes a spark of hope to ignite a fire within our students, and many of them are just one spark away from greatness. We can use our love to form connections and light that fire. Whether we invest in them every day, help them set life-changing goals, or assist them in forming forever friendships, we are rooting our impact in our love for them. Our impact makes us uNforgettable, and that status helps us motivate our learners to grow even more.

- **Reflect.** It can be tough to find time to demonstrate our love to every student we teach. Think about how you feel when someone you love shows you that you are important. Imagine being the one who offers that feeling to the kids who sit in front of you every day. Take a moment and ponder this question: Do your students know that they matter to you? What can you do to show them?

- **uNleash.** Make an investment. It is time to take action because every student deserves to feel important. Choose one of these three actions and uNleash a plan to make it happen this week.

1. Plan and prepare either a silent investment, a scheduled investment, or a public investment.

2. Check in with your students about something going on in their lives outside of school.

3. Identify isolated students and strike up conversations with them this week.

- **Get social:** Share how you demonstrated love for your students this week, and how you connected to them. Share "uNforgettable teachers love their students by _____" and fill in the blank, with the hashtag #WeTeachuN.

Stay Positive

*We need to make the positives
so loud that the negatives
are almost impossible to
hear.* — GEORGE COUROS

Destination Guide Three

IN THE CLASSROOM, OUR STUDENTS ARE RELYING ON US TO LEAD THEM INTO THE FUTURE. TO LEAD THEM, WE MUST BE CONFIDENT AND COMFORTABLE IN OUR OWN DECISIONS, STANDING STRONG AND CASTING A LIGHT INTO THE DARKNESS AHEAD.

uNveil Your Light

BE A BEACON.

A lighthouse is a beacon of light that serves two purposes. It offers sailors a navigational aid to help them fix their positions at sea, and provides a warning that there are dangerous areas nearby. This is the fixed point that steers sailors home and protects them as they navigate rough waters. We should aim to serve as a beacon of positivity, shining brightly even in the darkest of days. Our students need our aid as they navigate through life's ups and downs, and they will always look for the light that steers them home. Their days might be filled with the rough waters of learning difficulties, tough home lives, or simply rocky experiences before they step into our classrooms, but if we are consistent in our positivity, we can provide a light when they need it most.

An uNforgettable teacher is like a lighthouse in a number of ways. Such teachers believe in what they have to offer and are confident in the light that they're giving off. Although their confidence is high, they, too, are often surrounded by rough waters crashing into them from every angle. Standing up to these rough waters is difficult, and teachers who are constantly trying to stay positive may find that other people try to knock them down. Naysayers might question their ideas and spread doubt rather than supporting change.

Just like that lighthouse, you may be battered and beaten by the forces around you. Be brave enough to ignore the naysayers and stand tall in the face of adversity, the way lighthouses do, and you will set an example for your students about maintaining a light even in dark times. Stand out from the crowd and rise above the noise of negativity. Believe in your own foundation and your light and ignore the risks around you, and you will be able to serve your students in an uNforgettable way.

Staying Positive Will Provide a Strong Foundation

A house built on sand will likely slide and fall unless it's given a solid foundation. A house built on rock, however, will stand strong during even the toughest storms. It's the same with teaching; we need a firm base to stand on if we're going to keep from sliding around when the storms roll in. We must use our passion for students, our love of teaching, and the servant heart that dwells inside of us to build a strong foundation and ground us during those storms. A positive mindset can serve as the rock we need when negativity comes our way, and will offer freedom and confidence—which will then become contagious to our students. When we are sure of ourselves, we are better able to serve our students, but when we allow negativity to creep into our minds, we lose confidence and begin to question our abilities to connect and teach. We must start by grounding ourselves in a positive mindset so we can move forward with confidence. Students will take this confidence on as well, and run with it.

Staying Positive Will Provide Freedom

The first way to maintain a positive foundation is to avoid negativity at all costs. When we allow negativity to infiltrate our thinking, we give it permission to place handcuffs on our wrists and take away our freedom. Negativity can weigh heavily on our decisions by changing our teaching methods and trapping us behind the narrow-minded defense mechanism we know as fear. In that position, we will miss out on learning opportunities and strategies that could help our students learn in a more dynamic and effective way.

Staying positive, on the other hand, allows for forward movement. Many of the greatest breakthroughs in history have come from people who were not afraid to step past negativity and move forward into innovation. In the classroom, our students are relying on us to lead them into the future. To lead them, we must be confident and comfortable in our own decisions, standing strong and casting a light into the darkness ahead.

Adopting a positive mindset means we are freeing our minds to new ideas and skills. Whether it is a new technology, a social cue, or a content-specific skill, our goal must be to have a positive outlook when it comes to change. We must eliminate fear, and then lead by positive example. Our students will follow.

Staying Positive Will Provide Confidence

uNforgettable teachers understand that confidence is rooted in positivity and that it will impact their students in a major way. When we're confident, doubts turn into certainty, fear transforms into courage, and school becomes a place that students will never forget. Many of us have had moments when we experienced self-doubt and fear. Whether it happened when we were asked to take on a new subject, a new position, or simply a new student in the middle of the year, we may have found ourselves fearing the idea of failure.

Wouldn't it be something, though, if we could face those sorts of situations with positivity and confidence rather than a fear of change? We might transform our experience—and the experiences of our students. We will most certainly set an example of how to maintain strength and confidence in the face of a challenge.

You'll also find that this confidence is contagious. Students who know that they can rely on us because they've seen us take action to move things forward learn to have more confidence in us, and in themselves. Our goal is to help them anticipate success in all they do, but embrace failure as a detour that will lead them to the destinations they seek. If we allow negativity to creep into our lives, the detours become roadblocks, and the end goals start to seem impossible. However, we want to be the light in the dark. We want to show our students that they can be confident in all they do—if they approach every challenge with a positive outlook.

If we help them eliminate the self-doubt and fear, we become uNforgettable in their journeys.

uNravel a Plan to Shine Through the Storms and Stay Positive

Start by seeking ways to instill positivity into your own life. That positivity, once rooted, will spill over into your interactions with your students and colleagues. Take care of yourself to take care of those you teach. The first aspect of self-care lies in how you develop your mindset each day. Start each day with a plan in place to help you remain positive, even when tough situations present themselves, and make sure to use this plan whenever you're interacting with your students. When we are positive toward students, their memories of us, as well as our impact on them, will be positive as well. But how can we make sure that we remain consistently positive—enough so that we reach the status of uNforgettable?

EVERY TEACHER WANTS TO BE REMEMBERED WHEN STUDENTS REMINISCE ABOUT THEIR DAYS IN SCHOOL. WE WANT TO BE THE ONES WHO THEY COME BACK TO VISIT YEAR AFTER YEAR, AND WE WANT TO KNOW THAT WE MADE A DIFFERENCE IN THEIR LIVES.

We teach our kids to treat people how they would like to be treated, expect something wonderful each day, and to have faith that their futures are bright. If we want them to maintain those lessons in their lives, we have to show them how. A few simple methods are to greet them with a smile, an enthusiastic high-five, or a pat on the back for a job well done. Try a couple of these methods and you'll start a contagious wildfire of positivity. When we give them compliments in front of their peers, or remind them of how amazing they are when we pass them in the hallway, we show them how it feels to experience positivity. In doing so, we provide them with a template to follow, and they will mimic it any chance they get. One of the most beautiful things to see is when a student demonstrates positivity toward another student based on a seed you planted. This is uNforgettable.

Every teacher wants to be remembered when students reminisce about their days in school. We want to be the ones who they come back to visit year after year, and we want to know that we made a difference in their lives. When we take the time to train our minds to be positive, we will be able to leave a legacy that our students will remember. Maintaining that positive mindset requires consistency, but once you put yourself on that path, you'll find it easy to follow. The most difficult aspect of this process is knowing where to begin. Keep reading to discover easy methods for kick-starting a positive mindset.

Practice Gratitude

We have much to be thankful for, but we don't always take the time to reflect due to our busy schedules. Life gets in the way, and although we have many positive things going on, we often end up taking things for granted or missing moments altogether. When we reflect on what we are thankful for, we can make a big difference in our lives—and become better and more uNforgettable teachers. One step that we can take to maintain a positive mindset is to practice gratitude.

Here are three simple ways to get started:

Take action with the Thankful Three.

Teachers face a lot of expectations, and it's easy to become busy and forget to look at the world around us. Once we allow stress and overwhelm to rule our lives, everything spirals downward— and that carries over into our classrooms, and might even cause us to resent what we do each day. We might even start taking our frustrations out on our students and colleagues. If we aren't careful, people will start remembering us for all the wrong reasons. Eliminate that downward spiral before it begins by using the Thankful Three. All you have to do is remember these three phrases, and incorporate them into your life every day.

Make it a point to show gratitude to at least one peer and one student every day, for something they've done well or helped you realize. Give them a kind word, a note, or even a mention on social media! And don't forget to thank yourself, as well, for the hard work you are putting in. Take a moment to reflect and be grateful for what you bring to your class. You'll find yourself immediately becoming more positive, and you'll notice it coming out in a range of ways, from your tone of voice to the things that are happening around you—and particularly in your classroom.

THANK YOUR COLLEAGUES.
THANK YOUR STUDENTS.
THANK YOURSELF.

Set the example.

Create a checklist at the start of each week, and include simple tasks that will help you spread positivity among students and colleagues. These can be tasks like writing a note of appreciation to a student, calling a home to give parents praise about their child, or picking up bagels and coffee for a colleague. You can even extend the tasks to things that take place outside of school and on weekends. The goal is to be selfless and ask for nothing in return. It works this way:

1. Create the checklist at the start of the week, with a positive task assigned to each day, and keep it with you so you can keep track of what you have done.

2. Keep the same checklist every week, or change it up.

3. Complete one act each day, or all seven every day!

Performing small, simple acts of positivity will increase the morale of your students and faculty, and the negativity that normally surrounds you will change. We take care of responsibilities every day, and many of them go unnoticed, so imagine the reaction from your colleagues or students when you go out of your way to notice some of *their* actions. The more we take the time to appreciate each other with simple forms of gratitude, the better off the culture of the school will become. The positivity will spread, and everyone will start to feel better about what they're doing. Being the teacher that starts this chain reaction will forever cement you in the positive school culture.

Keep a gratitude journal.

People use journaling for many different reasons. Some artists will use it to document inspiration, busy entrepreneurs may use it to stay grounded, while others use it to reflect on their days. Regardless of the motivation, journaling is a proven way to release stress, meditate on topics, and remember important times in our lives.

We often lose positive experiences in the busyness of our daily lives. Journaling gives us a way to record those moments—and revisit them. We can refer back to those positive journals when times are tough, and use them to overcome our own self-doubt. Even more important, a gratitude journal will increase your positive mindset—and as we've already seen, that will spill over into our classrooms. When we take time each day to focus on what lifts us up, our approach to life will begin to shift, and we will become uNforgettably positive teachers. Follow these simple tips to get started:

Tips for Starting a Gratitude Journal

- Choose a journal (either paper or digital) and stick to it. If you enjoy typing or keeping notes on your phone, you may prefer digital journaling. If you want to slow down and take in the moment, then writing on paper is the way to go.

- Be consistent. Write in the journal every day at the same time. You can write as part of your morning routine, or before bed as your day winds down.

- Be simple and specific. Try to limit each entry to three things you are grateful for, and be specific about what they are. For example, instead of writing, "I'm grateful for my students," write, "I'm grateful for the kindness and appreciation my students showed me today when they…"

- Transform negative thoughts into positive affirmations. Use the negativity that may be bringing you down to lift you up instead. When writing in your journal, try to use "but statements." For example, you may write something like this: "Today I argued with a colleague, but I am grateful for how he challenges my thinking and makes me a better teacher for my students." The goal is to find the positive in a situation that may normally cause you to feel negative.

Ignore the Naysayers and Shine

The truth is, this is not easy, and you will come across days when it's difficult to stay positive. It is OK to have bad days, but it's also important to try to find *something* great in every day. Unfortunately, we may find resistance against that, as many people just enjoy being agitators. They don't know your heart, nor do they care about having a constructive dialogue with you. Instead, they seek only to be negative. These are the naysayers. You might find them to be colleagues or friends, or even the voice in your head that tries to destroy your confidence.

No matter who they are, you must find a way to ignore

them. When you allow others to influence you with their doubts, you step further away from being the teacher your students will remember, and closer toward self-doubt, frustration, and overwhelm. In order to be the light that your students need, you must find a way to shine in the midst of the naysayers. Start by surrounding yourself with positive people. We become better teachers when we have people around us lifting us up. Use the positivity we've been working on to eliminate the power of those negative influences and transfer your energy to focusing on what is best for your students, rather than worrying about what you need to do to please the doubters. Your ability to do this—to maintain that positivity—will make you uNforgettable.

The question remains, though: How do we handle the naysayers?

Don't Doubt Yourself

Sometimes, as a teacher, you can feel like you are running a marathon uphill. You doubt your vision, question your goals, and wonder if you have what it takes to teach. There are times when no matter how hard you try to move forward, you just feel as though you are stuck. During these times, you are facing your greatest naysayer: you. If you want to be an uNforgettable teacher, you must find a way to destroy the doubts that are holding you back from being who you were meant to be. Have confidence in your ideas and take risks. If you allow negative thoughts and people to sidetrack you, you may miss something important—and miss teaching it to your students.

uNforgettable teachers don't allow the negative influences to overtake their purpose. They know how to build a plan for positivity and take it into the day as a shield to block any negativity. They know that their positivity will also serve as a motivator for their students. Start every day with a positive mindset, and do whatever you must to give your students the best version of yourself, and you will become uNforgettable in their eyes.

uNleash Kindness and Give Thanks

Staying positive consistently takes work. Use personal discipline and dedication to achieve it, and you will give your students a place where they feel confident and free to engage in learning. Practice gratitude and ignore the naysayers to build a foundation of positivity that will spill over into your lessons. A teacher who has a positive mindset builds an atmosphere that invites students in, rather than scares them away. Do your best to shine your light every day, so you can guide students along a positive path and become uNforgettable.

- **Reflect:** Every day is a new day. You'll slip up and say or do things you regret on some days, but that doesn't mean you're not a positive force in the lives of your students. It just means you are human. Remember to be the best you can be for your students, and be as positive as possible in your responses to them. Start each day anew, and forget about past mistakes. Ponder the following questions as you move forward into being more positive for your students.

- When your students test your patience, do you remain firm, yet positive, in your responses to them, or do you lash out?

- What can you do today that will help you remain positive for your students during the good days as well as the tough ones?

- ## uNleash. Build a plan that sticks. Write a concise plan that you can refer back to when your confidence and positivity begin to slip. Read through the following three actions and write down one that you will uNleash this week.

  - Practice the Thankful Three starting tomorrow.

  - Create a checklist that you will complete this week to help you set an example of positivity.

  - Choose a gratitude journal and write your first entry.

- ## Get social. Thank a fellow teacher or colleague today. Share your gratitude with a post on social media using the hashtag #WeTeachuN.

Encourage Student Ownership

Tell me and I forget, show me and I may remember, involve me and I learn. — BENJAMIN FRANKLIN

Destination Guide Four

WE ARE THE GUIDES OUR
STUDENTS NEED TO HELP
THEM REACH PLACES
THEY NEVER DREAMED
POSSIBLE. WE HAVE THE
CHANCE TO HELP THEM
FEEL PROUD OF WHO THEY
ARE AND WHAT THEY DO.

uNveil the True Heroes

OUR STUDENTS ARE heroes.

The greatest stories tell of heroes who overcame the impossible and the mentors that guided them. Heroes go through many twists and turns, and must make tough decisions in order to succeed—and they almost always have mentors alongside them to provide wisdom and guidance. Although they share wisdom, the mentor also allows the hero to choose his or her own path. That way, the hero owns the outcome. Wise mentors understand that if heroes do not take ownership, then they are only taking orders, and for them to fulfill their destinies, they must be able to learn from their mistakes. Encouraging ownership is key to helping any hero learn, grow, and succeed.

Every student wants to be a hero. Students want to be the ones who feel special, and who others look at in a positive light. They want to make a difference in the world and stand for something bigger than themselves. The books they read and the movies they watch are filled with heroes who save the day, and our students want to emulate them.

Imagine if your classroom was filled with kids who viewed themselves as the heroes in their own stories. Now make that a reality. All your students need in order to achieve it is someone who is willing to guide them. As an uNforgettable teacher, you are a hero's mentor in disguise!

To be the best mentor possible, though, you have to teach your students how to take ownership of their own stories. Taking responsibility means they can learn and benefit from their hero's quest—and as a mentor, it's your job to show them the way. But what is ownership, and how do we teach it?

Ownership is personal. For example, there is a big difference between the things we rent and the things we own. When we rent a car, we aren't too concerned with what happens to it during the rental period. As long as we return it to the dealer with the minimum requirements satisfied, we will be happy. We don't provide special care or consideration for the cars we rent because we have no attachment to them. When we own a car, however, we take pride in how we care for it, because we've invested hard-earned money into it over time. It belongs to us, rather than to someone else, and we take pride in what we own. We do our best to keep it clean, change the oil, and maintain it so that it will last for years to come.

When we tell our students what to do without accepting input, or when we show them how to do something without allowing for exploration, it's the equivalent of them renting a car. They will go through the motions and provide the minimum requirements to accomplish what we ask of them, but they won't commit to it. When we involve them in the learning process, however, we offer them a chance to "buy" the car. We give them the opportunity to take ownership over the learning and make it their own.

uNforgettable teachers encourage students to take that step because they understand that with ownership comes pride and motivation to move forward toward success.

Student Ownership Provides Pride

If you have ever been to a school function where parents have the opportunity to watch their children perform, you know that there is nothing quite like watching the pride they display. They almost always have their phones out so they can film everything, and they make sure to let everyone around them know that the student on stage is "their kid." Yet when their child leaves the spotlight, they quietly go back to not paying much attention. The reason is simple: They are extremely proud of who they claim ownership of, and are merely polite toward everyone else.

Our goal is not to create polite students who quietly tune us out when it comes to school, but rather to create students who beam with pride when they see their learning in action.

Student ownership gives students a stake in their own education—and that provides them with pride. We are the guides our students need to help them reach places they never dreamed possible. We have the chance to help them feel proud of who they are and what they do. When we give them the opportunity to add to lessons based on their interests, we offer them value and a way to take pride in the learning.

Student Ownership Provides Motivation

In today's world, people are usually motivated in two ways. They are either externally motivated by things like money, trophies, or prizes, or they are internally motivated by something inside of themselves that drives them to improve. When people are motivated by the thought of a reward, they will always seek the finish line and an end to their movement. People who are internally motivated, however, are driven to raise the bar, and will always look for ways to make themselves better. They are invested in their goals on a totally different level. Our mission should be to help our students become lifelong learners who are motivated intrinsically, without the need for an external reward. We want to offer them something that drives them to move forward on their own and exceed expectations.

Student ownership provides that intrinsic motivation by making learning personal. We want to see our students loving the act of acquiring knowledge. When we give them ownership of their learning and make it something that they are invested in, we ignite that sort of passion. There is no greater reward than achieving a goal that we are invested in and passionate about. When we implement student ownership in our teaching, we change the game.

uNravel a Plan to Implement Student Voice and Ownership

The legend of King Arthur and his round table has been told for centuries. It is the story of a great king who valued the opinions of those he served. He held his meetings with his knights gathered around him, both so that he could hear their opinions and so they would know that he was listening to them with respect.

Although everyone looked to the king for answers, he allowed those at his table to share their thoughts and have a say in decisions. King Arthur understood that listening to the ideas and opinions of those he served made him a stronger leader.

When we implement student ownership in our classrooms, it is a lot like the legendary round table philosophy of King Arthur. Our students look to us for answers, and we lead them to the best of our abilities, but when we allow them to have input into their learning, we can serve them even better.

Giving up a little control within the classroom is a tough mindset shift, and it makes many teachers nervous. This is a natural response, but remember that when you push your own boundaries to reach into the unknown, you grow. When you embrace student ideas and opinions, you not only demonstrate respect but also show them that they are valuable. The Round Table Meeting is a quick way to get started in giving your students ownership over their learning.

The Round Table Meeting

Our students have amazing ideas. In some ways, they know more than we do when it comes to how they learn best. The Round Table Meeting strategy takes a page out of the legend of King Arthur and offers students a place at the teacher's table.

How It Works

Schedule a Round Table Meeting at the end of each unit of study. Allow approximately twenty minutes for the meeting (or whatever amount of time you think you need), and decide on a space in the classroom where the meeting will take place. Consistency and routine are key.

Step One: Open the meeting with reflection.

Prepare three open-ended questions to ask at the start of each meeting, and make sure they apply to the unit you've just finished. Sometimes I give the questions to students ahead of time so they can prepare answers. Here are a few sample questions:

- What is one thing we did this week that you enjoyed?

- What is one thing you really didn't enjoy this week in your learning? Explain why.

- What is one thing we learned this week that you found difficult? Explain why.

Take notes. It will take thick skin to hear their honesty, but it is crucial if you want the meeting to work.

Step Two: Ask for improvements.

Open the floor for students to give ideas on how the lessons from the week could have been improved.

- Keep a running list each week of student ideas.

- Share your thoughts with students as well, to spark discussion.

Step Three: Share the next unit of study and create a framework together.

- Once students have reflected and given their ideas for improvements, take a few minutes to plan a framework for the next unit of study.

- Share the topic or concept that they will be learning in the next unit or the next week.

- Ask them how they would like to journey through this unit. What strategies or ideas would they enjoy using as they embark on this learning journey?

- Based on their ideas, develop a framework for the unit to assist you in your planning.

- Optional ideas that work well in these meetings:

  - Give students a task to complete that adds to the unit of study, such as a rubric, assessment, or assignment.

  - Ask students to evaluate themselves and reflect on their personal performance for the week.

End the meeting with a two-minute recap

- End each meeting with a two-minute recap of what you discussed. Ask specific students to keep the "minutes" or notes for the meetings from time to time, and have them share as well.

- For most meetings, arrange for a student or two to give a quick summary of the reflection, the improvements, and the plan for the upcoming week. This way all students will be reminded of what you talked about and what is expected.

Let Students Evaluate You

Students will say things in the moment that can really sting. We have all been in a situation where a student put us down or hurt our feelings, and we had to set the example by being the bigger person. Everything inside of us wanted to lash out, but we were calm instead, simply diffusing the situation and moving on. It is all part of being a teacher, and yet another reason why we may be among the strongest people on the planet.

When it comes to helping students, thick skin is a must. That armor will help when we allow students to take more ownership in the classroom. It allows you to let them in and give them more input—and makes it easier to respond to their criticisms and see them as acts of collaboration rather than attacks. Truly uNforgettable teachers invite their students to take responsibility for the learning and handle the tough comments with grace and respect.

GIVING STUDENTS A CHANCE TO PROVIDE YOU WITH HONEST FEEDBACK WILL ALSO GIVE THEM AN EVEN DEEPER ATTACHMENT TO THEIR LEARNING. WHEN WE EXTEND A TRUSTING HAND AND ASK THEM FOR HELP, THEY GO FROM BEING THE RECEIVER OF KNOWLEDGE TO THE GIVER OF INSIGHT.

We are evaluated by administrators, supervisors, and colleagues. We don't always like it, and we sometimes disagree with the final analysis of our work, but when others evaluate us and we welcome their constructive points, we become better at our jobs. But there is something missing in this system because the most important people in the room never get to do the evaluating. Our students see us every single day. They experience the "bells and whistles" we put into some lessons, as well as the daily grind. They are the ones who can truly help us become better teachers with their input. Opening yourself to student critique is not easy, but it will help you impact them in an even greater way.

Giving students a chance to provide you with honest feedback will also give them an even deeper attachment to their learning. When we extend a trusting hand and ask them for help, they go from being the receiver of knowledge to the giver of insight. They become invested in the relationship between teacher and student, and this type of ownership is powerful. uNforgettable teachers are willing to put their pride on the line in order to make the students' experience amazing. Here are three simple strategies for allowing student evaluation in your classroom.

Three Simple Ways
for Students to Evaluate You

Evaluation Strategy One: The weekly secret survey

One thing that guarantees honesty is anonymity. Create a simple, three-question Secret Survey that students can take at the end of the week that does not ask for their names. Make sure that at least one question has a scale or form of measurement to help guide them (I personally use emojis they can circle to demonstrate their opinion, but a scale of 1–10 can work). One or two open-ended questions are always a good idea as well. Three questions I have used that seem to work well are:

- How did I do this week as your teacher?

- What is one thing I could have done better this week?

- What is one thing I can do to challenge you or make your experience in class better?

Using three questions means students can answer quickly, and further ensures that it won't take long to go through their feedback. Once you've taken their comments on board, decide how you can implement their feedback.

Seeing their feedback taken seriously will help students take ownership of the class. They will no longer look at the classroom relationship as one-sided. Rather, they will view their learning experience as a journey that they are actively helping to construct.

Evaluation Strategy Two: The ticket out

When we end our lessons, we often use some form of quick evaluation or "ticket out" to make sure our students grasped the concept we taught that day. A great way to mix things up and get immediate feedback from students on how the lesson went is an Evaluation Ticket Out. Create a ticket out (could be a small slip of paper or something using online technology) that focuses on how you did with teaching that day. You can include generic questions focusing on what they understood and what they missed, or you can cater specifically to the concepts you taught. Use a scaling system or a grading system to simplify their feedback. Students love to grade their teachers, and often do a fantastic job. Here are two sample questions you can use, but the sky's the limit with this evaluation strategy:

- If you had to grade me on today's lesson, what would I receive in these areas and why?

- On a scale of 1–10 (1 being "I'm totally lost" and 10 being "I get it!"), how would you rate your understanding of today's lesson and how I presented the material? Why?

Evaluation Strategy Three: The quarterly report

Businesses often give quarterly reports to show how successful they have been, or how they have missed the mark. As a teacher, you can take this strategy and put the power into your students' hands. Give them the opportunity to create this report, and the chance to create change for the better. This is usually a power only the "boss" gets to have. At the end of each quarter, have your students create a quarterly report covering three areas. Ask them to break down each area in detail, and give them time to create the report. I usually have my students complete this report at home at the end of each marking period, and return it to me when they are ready.

- **Area One:** Teacher clarity (How well did students understand what was being taught?). In this section, students comment on teaching strategies and what worked or didn't work. They can give suggestions on how to improve and encourage things that they'd like to see continue.

- **Area Two:** Class atmosphere (How conducive was the atmosphere for learning?). In this section, students can comment on the class itself. They can give suggestions about how to set up the classroom for a better learning experience.

- ## Area Three: Relationships (How comfortable are the students in the class itself? Do they feel safe asking questions or exploring their learning?). In this section, students can comment on how you make them feel as students. They can give you suggestions on how to build more trust, or how to go about making deeper connections with them.

When we allow students to evaluate us, we give them ownership that extends beyond their seats. We are guaranteeing that we will hear their voices. This shows that we're building a culture of collaboration and a classroom that is filled with owners rather than passive consumers. When we own something, we are invested in it, whether it is a car or a classroom. When students own their learning and are able to give input on how they learn best, they will be invested in what they have helped to create.

uNleash Learning and Break the Mold

Student ownership provides pride and motivates them to commit to their learning. They will never forget a teacher who gives them that sort of power. Plan with your students instead of around them, and make sure you're encouraging open dialogue about the learning process. More than anything, students want to be heard. They have an inner desire to feel valued. When we open the door for them to give input into their learning, and use their suggestions to better their experience, school becomes important to them. Student ownership is one of the most powerful tools at a teacher's disposal because it demonstrates, in a tangible way, that student opinions matter.

- **Reflect.** Sometimes the most engaging lessons are the ones that students design themselves. Although we are the guides who will bring knowledge and insight, students are the best witnesses when it comes to whether or not they're grasping the concepts. As you reflect on student ownership within your own classroom, use these questions to help guide you:

  - How often do you listen to what your students have to say?

  - Do you hear them and act on their behalf, or do you decide what is best for them regardless of their opinions?

  - What can you do to help them give input into their learning?

- **uNleash.** Choose one thing you want to change right away. Implementing student ownership doesn't require an entire teaching shift. It just takes a few small steps to begin a learning transformation in the classroom. The following two actions will help you begin the process. Write down one that you will uNleash this week, and commit to carrying it out.

- Schedule a Class Round Table and prepare three questions to ask during the meeting.

- Create an Evaluation Ticket Out or a Secret Survey to give to your students this week.

- ## Get social: Share one way that teachers can encourage student ownership. Spread your message by posting it on social media using the hashtag #WeTeachuN.

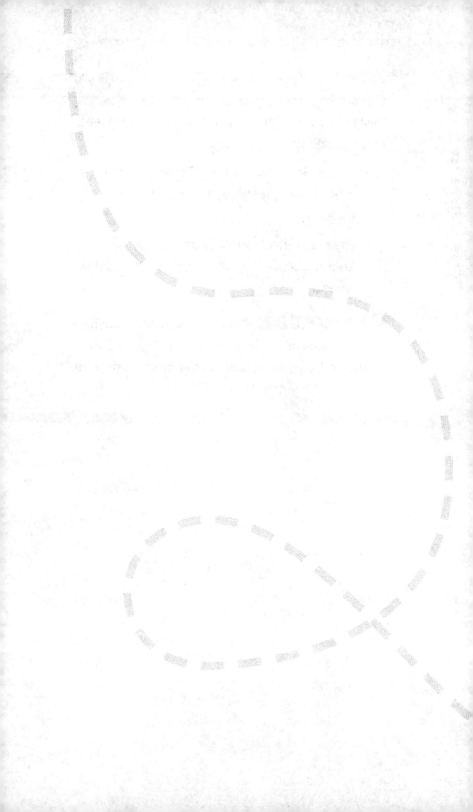

Embrace Failure

Success consists of going from failure to failure without loss of enthusiasm. — WINSTON CHURCHILL

Destination Guide Five

STUDENTS REMEMBER
THE TEACHERS WHO
WERE HONEST WITH
THEM WHEN THEY
MADE MISTAKES, AND
WHO DEALT WITH
THOSE MISTAKES
GRACEFULLY.

uNveil Your Struggles and Successes

YOU WILL MAKE mistakes, and that is OK. It is in our nature to learn from the failure that accompanies those mistakes. When we are babies, we learn to walk by falling over again and again. With every stumble comes insight, and with each fall comes a lesson that brings us closer to our first steps. Rather than giving up, we choose to be persistent, and after countless failures, we succeed. Once we have mastered our first steps, we learn to run, climb, and explore. Being new at this, we continue to stumble. We fall and scrape our knees, but wander into the unknown without fear because we know our parents are close behind, following us to make sure we stay safe.

Developing means failing in order to learn from our mistakes. When we're first starting out, the key is having smiling parents in front of or behind us, following us closely with arms outstretched. They show us through their enthusiasm that our missteps are OK, that our stumbles are just temporary, and that with each fall we gain the knowledge we need to move forward.

Sometimes our students struggle because they are merely learning to "walk" when it comes to their education. Some take longer to balance, some will fall more than others, and some will persistently stumble. We can help all students achieve their full potential by guiding them along that path. We need to be the ones who believe in them slightly more than they believe in themselves, and teach them that "failure" is not a bad word.

uNforgettable teachers fail often, as well—and that is why we succeed. We teach lessons that just don't work, and our classroom management practices are filled with blunders. When our patience is tested, we sometimes lash out in frustration, rather than love, and we even take part in the gossip that surrounds us in the hallway or faculty room. We fail in these ways, and many more, because we are human.

But to succeed through those failures, we must learn to take the right steps afterward—both for ourselves and for our students. It's OK to make mistakes, as long as we own them and learn from them. From the mistake itself, we take baby steps forward until we become a little braver … and learn to take more risks. If a lesson fails, we figure out why it didn't work and risk trying something new to reach our students. When we have a moment of weakness, whether with a colleague or a student, and we say something we regret, we humble ourselves in order to repair the relationship—and learn not to do it again.

And though we may feel like failures, particularly when we make these mistakes in front of our students, the truth is that students remember the teachers who were honest with them when they made mistakes, and who dealt with those mistakes gracefully.

The road great teachers travel on is not a smooth one. It is filled with potholes, detours, and sharp turns. We have to learn to navigate our own obstacles on our personal teaching journeys, not only so we grow as teachers, but so we can guide our students on *their* journeys. In time, we learn how to overcome the roadblocks, navigate the detours, and recognize the turns that once surprised us. That success depends on us learning from our failures, though, and to do that successfully we must change our mindsets. Instead of being afraid of failure, embrace the idea of "failing forward"—and teach your students to do the same.

Unfortunately, we often view failing as negative, because that's what we've been told since we were young. But we must change this view in ourselves, and help our students to change it as well. When we refuse to let our mistakes define us, we lose the fear of failure—and we pass that bravery on to those we teach. When our students stop being afraid to make mistakes, they will become free to explore their learning and will have the opportunity to grow.

This mindshift change must begin with us. Do not focus on what failure takes away. Instead, look forward to the wisdom and growth it provides. Learn to overcome the stigma that surrounds failure, so you can offer your students the freedom to learn from their mistakes as well. It will make you, in their eyes, truly uNforgettable.

Failure Provides Wisdom

When we were children, our parents were there to guide us when we made mistakes. Without that guidance, we would have gone astray. As we grow beyond our childhood homes, we choose new people to offer us wisdom and guidance— people who have experienced things we wish to accomplish, or who have made the mistakes we hope to avoid. We look to them for coaching during tough times and when we're making decisions. Sometimes we turn to coaches who train us, or veterans in the fields in which we hope to make our careers. No matter who they are, we look to mentors for their wisdom. These people have gained knowledge through their experiences and failures, and that qualifies them to offer life advice to others.

Mentors have used their own failures to increase their knowledge of life, and when we do the same, we, too, grow into mentors. We begin to look at failure through a big-picture lens and view our past experiences and mistakes as teaching moments from which we can guide our students. We use these moments to teach them life lessons that they will remember for the rest of their lives. Sometimes, the most important lessons we teach our students come from the wisdom we have acquired, rather than the textbooks we are given.

Instead of fearing failure, welcome the wisdom that comes with it, and learn to use that wisdom to serve your students. In turn, you will become the uNforgettable teacher they look to when they need help.

Failure Provides Growth

Failure also provides the opportunity for growth. When we fail at something, we are given two choices: either accept it … or use it as a springboard for growth and work hard to defeat it. The key lies in belief. It is a lot easier to believe in ourselves when we have other people believing in us as well.

To our students, failure can be a dream killer or it can be dream fuel, depending on how we present it. When they believe failure to be negative, experiencing it will stunt their growth and cause them to give up. When, however, they experience it as an opportunity to grow and move forward, they will see failure as a chance to cross one thing off the list of options and explore new directions. Instead of seeing it as a defeat, they'll embrace it as a challenge.

The biggest difference is whether or not they have someone standing behind them, telling them they can achieve anything. We become uNforgettable teachers when we're the ones standing behind them. When we help our students grow through their failures, and guide them as they make mistakes, we can keep them on the path of excellence. We have the power to help our students grow through failure—if we fuel the fire they have inside them.

Teachers essentially fall into one of two categories: those who see failure as draining or those who see it as exhilarating.

- Those who see student failure as draining will comfort their students after they fail at something and then encourage them to find another area where they might be more successful. They look at failure as an endpoint, and will not attempt to help a student improve where they have already failed. They will instead encourage the student to avoid the area—and in doing so, they discourage challenge and learning.

- Those who see failure as exhilarating will encourage students to learn from their mistakes and will push them to master what they failed at in order to grow. These teachers encourage students to develop a growth mindset and understand that each mistake leads to a possibility of improving.

Although it may be easier to look at failure as an endpoint, it is more beneficial to students to show them that failure is just an opportunity for growth. It may take more time and patience to have an exhilarating mindset when it comes to failure, but it is worth it in the long run. Our students will adopt the mindset we guide them toward, and when we offer them growth instead of limitations, we become uNforgettable.

uNravel a Plan to Teach Students to Fail Forward

Failure can often feel like trying to walk up a downward-moving escalator. Think about what would happen if you tried this. It would be a struggle to make your way from one end to the other. First, people would be frustrated with you and would make comments about how annoying you were. Second, with the moving conveyor belt of steps under your feet pushing you in the opposite direction, you would only be able to move forward a little bit at a time, and it would take forever to make progress. Eventually, you would have to make a choice to either push through and make it to the top, or stop altogether and move backward.

That's what our students go through when they fail. No matter how hard they try, things just don't seem to move forward. Frustration sets in and they eventually reach a crossroads where they either give up or push through. If they feel alone at the crossroads, they will assume that they are not good enough for this challenge and quit. They will refuse to break down barriers because, in their minds, they just aren't smart enough.

When we walk with them, though, we can help them through those barriers. We become the ally they seek and give them the confidence to make it to the top. We must show them that the journey is just as important as the destination and that they can push through the failure. Use the following suggestions to start changing your students' views of failure and encouraging them to push through the crossroads to reach the top of that escalator.

Erase the Labels

Start by changing the concept of labels for people. Labels are good for boxes and containers because they tell us what's inside. But people don't fit into boxes—yet we often treat them that way. We label them with letters, acronyms, and in some cases, preconceived notions, before they enter our classrooms. These labels follow them through their school career and eventually begin to define who they are. Two of the most common labels have to do with how students define themselves as learners, and how they view themselves as people. Help them erase these labels and you will start a chain reaction and put them on a path toward a label-free life.

- **The letter-grade label.** This is the learning label students give themselves, and it usually starts with a definition from a teacher or parent. We need to measure our students' learning, and in most cases, we use letters to help define their progress. This, however, puts too much emphasis on the letter itself, and not enough on the actual learning going on. If students are trained to view success through the lens of a letter, and they define themselves by those grades, then their motivation for learning becomes a limiting goal rather than limitless learning. When they fail to achieve that letter-grade goal, they count themselves as failures and quit trying.

  This label, then, does more harm than good.

  Erase the label by placing the emphasis on the process rather than the grade. Assess students as they move through the material and break the content down into smaller chunks to help them understand concepts better. Instead of the goal to master a test, focus on students mastering the concepts they are learning about. If you are able to go gradeless and focus on assessing students differently, do so. If your district does not allow this, input "grades" that reflect mastery, and focus only on what demonstrates learning. If students forget to put their names on their papers, are too talkative during an assignment, or are misbehaving during instruction, deal with the problems accordingly, but do not mark them off entirely. These things do not reflect their mastery of a concept. If students do not under-stand a concept, allow them to try again, and work with them until they master the learning to their full potential before moving forward.

The key to erasing the letter-grade label is changing our mindsets about learning. We need to worry less about the average our students end up with on a report card if we want them to become above average. We need to allow them to grow through the struggle so they understand that the grade doesn't matter as much as their reaction to failure and challenge. Teachers who present this lesson become truly uNforgettable to their students.

- **The behavior label.** This is the label that judges students based on who they are as people. Many of our students are labeled as troublemakers before they ever set foot in our classrooms. They come with baggage because somewhere along the way they were marked as a problem, and that label stuck with them. Many of our students define themselves as a troubled student because they have been labeled that way by their teachers. Unfortunately, the label affects not only the way teachers treat them, but also the students' ideas about themselves.

Erase this label by giving those students attention that breaks the mold. When students act up, they are often looking for attention. If the attention they receive reinforces the label that has been placed on them, nothing will change. If, however, we address their behavior differently, we can change their lives. When students misbehave, give them an appropriate consequence for their actions, but make this the first step rather than the endpoint. Follow up by allowing them to tell you their story and by becoming a mentor. They may not need consequences or discipline at all. Many of them simply need someone who is willing to listen. They need someone to hear their side of the story, even if they were completely in the wrong. When we become that person for them, we become uNforgettable, and help them to see that they are not limited by a label that others have put on them.

These are just two examples of labels, but we have the chance to address all labels in this way. Removing the labels inside the classroom will help students remove the labels they experience outside of the classroom as well. Sometimes all it takes is removing one label for the rest to be set free. Give your students the chance to start over, free of labels, and you'll make yourself an important part of their foundation.

Know the Context

We must look at the context of the situation and see the bigger picture. When you have students who do poorly due to lack of motivation or effort, find out why, and build relationships with them. Oftentimes, they believe that their worth is found in their "label," and don't care about school because school never cared about them. Some of our most intelligent students fail our classes, not because they can't do the work, but because they need something more. They need to know that they matter, in order to take what we are teaching seriously. They may be those students who refuse to do anything in class and therefore end up failing, or they may be the ones who rush through just to get things done. Either way, they have a reason for acting that way, and if we fail to find that context, we fail them.

We may have students who have had a bad morning or are struggling with something personal. Their struggles might reflect in their behavior, but before assuming that they are acting out of disrespect or that they are lazy or unmotivated, find out why they're acting that way. Serve them by asking the question first. There is a big difference between an F on a report card and a student who fails. Stop looking at the labels and figure out the context of the situation. Your toughest students might be your smartest kids. They might just need someone to put effort into showing them the right path. Become the teacher who takes the time to look at the whole picture and consider the context before drawing a conclusion, and you will leave an imprint that lasts forever.

Tell Your Own Failure Stories

Students love to hear personal stories about their teachers, and you can keep this tool at your fingertips to help you connect with your students. When we delve into our personal lives, it gives our students the chance to see us as real people. When they see that we make mistakes in our lives, they will feel more comfortable doing the same in theirs. Use the power of the story to teach them that failure is a good thing. Share the small failures that you have each day, as well as the larger ones that have helped you become who you are. We live in an instant-gratification society where our students expect things to come quick and easy. We must teach them that success through failure often requires time. We cannot expect them to have grit and determination to see things through if they don't understand the concept of delayed gratification. Use personal stories of perseverance and resilience to demonstrate the importance of grit, and you will reach them more successfully.

When you implement these stories into your teaching, they become part of the lesson. Give students time to connect with the stories you tell, and then ask them to share their own personal stories. Offer your own experiences first, and then connect them to theirs, and you'll give them a way to see how failure can lead to success. Sometimes our students need to hear our stories and see our examples before they are brave enough to share and learn from their own.

Reset the Table

The beauty of dinner at home with family is that no matter what happens during one dinner, whether the conversation is great or it takes a turn for the worse, there is always the chance to reset the table and start again tomorrow. Our students are family, and they should feel that way in our classrooms. They should always have a chance to reset the table and start again when they fail. If you have students who fail a test or an assignment, give them the chance to reset and try again. Sometimes all they need is a second chance. If they fail in behavior or in other areas within your class, don't equate failure with a penalty, but rather with a goal. Provide them with small, measurable goals that will lead them to success in that area, then allow them to reset the table and begin again. Students will start to realize that failing at something is a step toward learning to do it successfully, instead of a step back from something impossible to achieve.

Empower Your Students

Video games are popular with students because failure is just a step toward the end, rather than an endpoint. It's not easy to get to the end, but if students are willing to fail enough times—and learn from those failures—they'll eventually achieve success. When they first begin playing, the goal seems unattainable. They take the challenge, though, because small successes are handed out along the way. They will spend hours failing on one level just so they can move forward to the next level once they figure it out. With each misstep, they learn how to correct their mistakes in order to move forward.

The secret to the success of video games lies in the combination of success and failure together. With every failure comes a little success, and with enough failure comes victory.

Reimagine your class as a video game, where students who are willing to fail enough times will win in the end. Instead of teaching them to view missteps and failures as negatives, teach them to see them as stepping stones toward success. Give your students the opportunity to fail so they can figure things out. When we give them the answer to every question, they don't learn—and they definitely won't move to the next level on their own. Offer them instead the independence they need to find their own way to get from A to B, and let them fail along the way. Serve as the "cheat codes" when they need you, to help them move when they are stuck, but allow them to struggle. They will learn more from the challenge in front of them if they have to figure it out themselves, as opposed to having the answers just given to them. And learning on their own will give them ownership of their journeys.

It will, in effect, empower them and improve their confidence.

Take the model of the video game as your inspiration, and model your lessons after the levels students have to overcome to succeed in the game. Create lessons that challenge students enough so that they make progress by accomplishing a little bit more each time—but failing every so often, as well. This should be a progression rather than a one-stop trip. When you allow them to fail in a positive way, they will grow and learn more than you ever thought possible.

Think about the many times you have failed in life. As

teachers, we make mistakes almost every day, and we learn from them. Many of us have been lucky enough to have someone guide us through our mistakes and help get us back on track. uNforgettable teachers do that for their students. They don't make students feel small for not understanding concepts, but instead provide positive feedback and demonstrate how their mistakes help them grow. It might not be easy or simple to embrace failure, but in the end, it will be an essentially important lesson for your students. When students leave your room equipped with the confidence to fail, they will have one of the most important tools they need to succeed.

uNleash Failure Without Fear

Failure is the stepping stone to success. When we teach our students that it's OK to make mistakes, and when we embrace failure ourselves in their presence, we teach them a life lesson that will stick with them forever. Take the time to help them erase the labels others have given them, and you will show them that they are not defined by letters or the opinions of others. Allow them to reset the table as many times as they need to so that they become empowered to fail in order to succeed. Do that, and you will become an uNforgettable force in their lives.

- **Reflect.** When we can embrace our own failures, we can help guide our students when *they* make mistakes. Reflect on your own life: How do you handle failure? Do you feel embarrassed or ashamed … or do you own it? How can you become better at embracing failure this week, and helping your students to do the same?

- **uNleash.** Practice embracing failure. We must be intentional about recognizing our mistakes in order to learn from them. If we want to guide our students through their failures, we must first figure out how to do it. It's not easy to be the guide for our students, but they desperately need us to fill this role. The following two actions will help you reflect on your own failures, and give you a pattern for helping your students through theirs. Decide to uNleash one of them this week, and commit to carrying it out.

  - Write down one mistake you have made this week, and record what you have learned from it and how you plan to do better next time.

  - Choose one of the five strategies in this chapter and implement it this week with a student who is struggling.

- **Get social.** Almost every success comes from failure. Share a success story from your life or teaching career. Be creative and post it on social media using the hashtag #WeTeachuN.

Find Balance

Life, like surfing, is all about wave selection and balance. Never let the best waves in life go by. — ANONYMOUS

Destination Guide Six

WE'RE OFTEN FACED
WITH THE FACT
THAT THERE'S NOT
ENOUGH TIME IN THE
DAY TO ACCOMPLISH
EVERYTHING.
ACHIEVING BALANCE
WILL HELP TO SOLVE
THIS CONUNDRUM
SINCE BALANCE
WILL FREE US FROM
UNNECESSARY
RESPONSIBILITIES.

uNveil True Balance

FINDING BALANCE IS not easy, but it is worth it.

Professional surfers have balance. They have the remarkable ability to stand on a board without falling off while powerful waves continually attempt to knock them down. They understand that in order to stay upright, they have to control their own actions, rather than letting the waves beneath them control the situation. They learn to respect the power of the ocean and just enjoy the ride.

As teachers, our work can sometimes feel like a wave crashing beneath our feet and trying to knock us off balance. We become so overwhelmed with lesson plans, expectations, and initiatives that we have little time to enjoy anything else at all, and our job becomes more of a burden than a labor of love. We feel as though we are surfers who just can't stay upright, and we find ourselves falling into the ocean time and time again. Finding a way to balance is the only way to keep from drowning. When we find balance, our vision becomes clear and we are able to rise above the waves and make an even greater impact.

uNforgettable teachers understand the importance of balance. Although we find ourselves falling from time to time, we follow a plan and maintain a set of boundaries that show us the line between our surfboard and the raging ocean around us. The plan and the boundaries give us a path to follow, even when things become a struggle. It's easy to get consumed by what's going on in the moment, but a plan keeps us on the path toward success, and the grander scheme of things.

Together, a plan and boundaries can give us the balance we require to succeed. So where do we start finding our balance? First, we work to understand why it's so important.

Finding balance is similar to going on a diet. Most diets fail because people are looking for a short-term fix to help them lose a few pounds. After the diet ends, they go back to eating the same foods that made them gain weight in the first place, and the cycle continues. If they want a diet to be successful over a long period of time, they have to alter their lifestyles and shift their mindsets, as well as change their food choices. Finding balance is similar. We all want to create a better balance between life and work, but when we only look for the quick fix, we implement strategies blindly, without figuring out a long-term plan. We might achieve short-term bliss that way, but eventually, we will fall back into overwhelm.

For us to achieve a truly balanced lifestyle, we have to go deeper than just putting together a strategy or two. We must change the way we *think*. We must also realize that we have to achieve that balance if we're going to be effective in the classroom—and in life itself. When we spend too much time worrying about what is happening in our classroom, our home life will suffer. If we cannot handle the responsibilities outside of work, our students will be affected. Without proper balance, we spiral into frustration and overwhelm, and it inevitably spills into our interactions with others.

The key lies in accepting how important planning and balance are to our lives. Once we understand and accept that importance, we can start on our plan for achieving the balance we seek—and we can move toward becoming uNforgettable teachers with plenty of time for our students.

Finding Balance Provides Time

We're often faced with the fact that there's not enough time in the day to accomplish everything. Achieving balance will help to solve this conundrum since balance will free us from unnecessary responsibilities. What would you do with more time in your classroom? I bet you have a whole list of things! Teachers want to complete amazing projects with their students and offer life-changing learning experiences, but a lack of time often seems to get in the way. A common belief is that if we had more hours in the day, we would accomplish everything we set out to do. But time itself is not the factor that holds us back. Rather, it is the lack of a plan or boundaries that causes us to feel overwhelmed. When we take on too many responsibilities, we become unbalanced—and more forgettable. To be completely uNforgettable, we need to learn to find that balance again, so that we can be the teachers our students need.

Have you ever wondered how some people find time to plan remarkable lessons, give consistent feedback to their students, collaborate with colleagues, and enjoy plenty of time with family and friends? They do not have more hours than anyone else; they simply have a plan in place and set boundaries that they stick to without excuses. When we are balanced, we have more time. Instead of making excuses as to why we can't accomplish something, we need to take action and actively pursue balance in order to give us the time we so desperately seek.

Finding Balance Provides Perspective

Balance can also provide us with perspective by uncovering our blind spots. Blind spots are areas or opportunities that we miss due to our busy schedules and hectic day-to-day lives. Sometimes we get so caught up in the things we are doing that our joy passes us by.

In today's classrooms, things change so rapidly that it can be difficult to keep up. Our schools are constantly giving us new lessons to try, and we are bombarded each year with a new learning theory that will revolutionize our teaching. If we aren't careful, keeping up with our jobs in the classrooms can take over our entire lives, and we will forget about those who are sitting right in front of us.

When we have a healthy balance between our work and our life outside of work, however, we will be able to see more clearly. We will be able to slow down in the moment to address student needs and build relationships with them. With the right perspective, we can inspire our students to grow, because we will be moving forward ourselves. When we are balanced, we will experience the things we didn't realize we were missing, reduce our stress in tough times, and dive into making a difference in the lives of those we teach.

uNravel a Plan to Have Work-Life Balance

Teachers plan.

If there is one thing that teachers do well, it's planning. We know how to organize every minute of instructional time so students don't miss a moment of learning. We can prepare units of study weeks before teaching them, and we are masters at getting the most out of the short time we have with our students. Despite our planning prowess, though, many of us lose track of the idea once we transition out of our school mindsets and into our personal lives. We often build a lopsided lifestyle, where the heaviest amount of time remains on one side. When we don't take the time to explore our own passions and interests, we drain ourselves and end up exhausted because there is too much on our plate. We become resentful and bitter, and cannot possibly serve our students well. If we are looking to be the teachers they never forget, we have to find a way to balance that out.

To find balance, we must address how we spend our time, the boundaries we set, and the goals we expect to meet each day. To start, work on managing your energy, setting your priorities, creating a time budget, signing a boundary contract, and following the daily Rule of Threes. Let's start with managing your energy.

Manage Your Energy

Peak seasons for theme parks and vacation destinations are determined by how busy they are at a specific time of year. Their peak season is when they are most productive as a business. Our personal peak time can be viewed in the same way. Some people are most productive in the morning, while others do their best work at night. *Your* peak time is when you have the most energy to complete a task—and you work the most efficiently.

Identify your peak time to help you start to build balance in your life and teaching. When you consider your usual day, when is it easiest for you to work, and when do you feel the most efficient? On average, people have three to five peak hours in a day, so pay attention to the tasks that require the most energy, and accomplish those during your peak hours. Use your not-so-peak hours to accomplish the tasks that take less concentration or motivation. Doing these important—and perhaps most difficult—tasks during these hours will guarantee that you get them done, and leave the rest of the day for lesser tasks that take less energy and focus.

You will find that your days are more organized and that you end up getting more done. We often spend too much time trying to figure out how to fit everything into the limited amount of time we have each day, and end up failing at many of our goals. If, though, we figure out when our energy is at its highest point, and budget our time with that in mind, we can increase our effectiveness and efficiency.

Here's an example of how I work to manage my energy throughout the day:

High-energy time (5–8 a.m., 3–5 p.m.): Spend time with family, write podcast episodes and blog posts, brainstorm ideas for the uNseries

Mid-energy time (11 a.m.–1 p.m.): Plan lessons, grade papers, collaborate with colleagues

Low-energy time (6–9 p.m.): Work out, read/answer email, watch TV, check social media

Follow these simple steps to help you match your energy level with the proper task:

- Step One: Consider which tasks take up most of your energy. If you're struggling, try creating a list or chart and classifying your tasks in regard to how difficult they are.

- Step Two: Determine when you are at your best during the day; when you have the most energy. For some teachers, this will be in the morning or during a prep period. For others, it may come at the end of a school day, after the students have left the building.

- Step Three: Plan to complete your high-energy tasks during your peak hours.

- Step Four: Complete your mid-energy tasks during other times of the day, when you still have energy, but are outside or at the edges of your peak time. These tasks might include things like grading papers, completing paperwork, or planning units with colleagues.

- Step Five: Leave your low-energy tasks for the time of day when you have the least energy. These are the things that take the least mental work and can be left for times when you have the least mental energy. Include things like checking email, social media, or working out.

WHEN WE MANAGE OUR ENERGY, WE FIND THE REMAINING HOURS IN THE DAY LESS STRESSFUL. WE WILL BE ABLE TO FULLY FOCUS ON MEANINGFUL MOMENTS, AND OUR STUDENTS WILL APPRECIATE THE UNDIVIDED ATTENTION.

We often become frustrated by everything that is expected of us on a daily basis. Although we accept the challenges with open arms, we are still human, and pressures can take a toll on us. Manage your energy to combat this problem—and to make you more productive and effective in the classroom. Teachers with more energy and efficiency have more time to try new things, and more energy to put toward mentoring their students. When we manage our energy, we find the remaining hours in the day less stressful. We will be able to fully focus on meaningful moments, and our students will appreciate the undivided attention.

Once you take the time to sync your energy and your tasks, you find that you not only achieve more balance in your life, but get things done efficiently, and then have more time to invest in students, friends, and family. If you want to make learning memorable for your students, you have to be fully present when things happen. When you're so overwhelmed that you have trouble paying attention to your students, it means you're not fully present—potentially when a student needs you the most. Be the teacher who is paying attention when a student needs you, and you'll become uNforgettable. Managing your energy will help you create a balance between the classroom and your home life, and will allow you to leave a lasting impression on everyone in your world.

Set Your Priorities: The 80-Percent Principle

If you want to manage your energy and get the most out of your day, you have to let go of a few things. When it comes to our teaching, we consider everything in our classroom as important. Everything has its place, from our set-up to where we store the pencils for our students. The truth is, though, that some of the things we worry about have little to do with student success, and the more time we spend focusing on these things, the less time we have to invest in our students. Ultimately, we only have a set amount of time each day, and we'll get more done with it if we let go of the less important things and prioritize our time.

To start your journey with balancing your time, try the 80-percent principle: Spend 80 percent of your time on the activities that produce 80 percent of the results you hope to achieve. For example, if you want to create a student-centered classroom, spend 80 percent of your time on gathering student input, seeking help from students with the planning, and figuring out how to teach based on their needs. Spend the other 20 percent of the time adapting those findings into individual lessons. If your goal is to build better relationships with your students, spend 80 percent of your allotted time guiding their learning, getting to know them personally, and creating an atmosphere that makes them feel safe enough to learn. Spend the other 20 percent of your time on collaboration or bonding with colleagues to improve your overall teaching style.

Using the 80-percent principle will allow you to focus your energy on the core of your goal. This is a tough balance for teachers because we think we need to give 100 percent of our time to everything that is thrown at us. To accomplish that, we often waste time on things that do not produce the outcomes we are looking for, and then grow frustrated and unbalanced. Prioritize your time using the 80-percent principle to avoid that pitfall, and you will see better results in more important areas, which will lead to better growth in student academic achievement and personal improvement.

Set Your Personal Priorities

When it comes to finding balance in your life, you must start with your priorities. Categorize these into three different areas: personal, career, and influence.

- Your personal priorities have to do with personal relationships, family, health, and wellness.

- Your career priorities are related to your teaching responsibilities, as well as activities that help you grow and advance as a teacher.

- Your influence priorities help increase your overall influence and impact. These may include mentoring new teachers, encouraging others through your blog or social media, and creating curriculum.

Your main priorities should fit into one of these three categories. Use the 80-percent rule to address your own unique priorities to establish a time budget (see the next section). We've all come across a colleague who was able to nurture relationships with students, develop creative lessons, and head up committees to help school culture thrive, all while finding time for things they enjoyed outside of school. We often look at these people as superhuman, but the truth is that they may just be super organized when it comes to time and priorities. We don't need to feel overwhelmed by a full schedule or packed calendar; we just need to prioritize things well and get rid of the time-wasting tasks that creep into our lives. uNforgettable teachers always seem to find a way to get things done while putting their students first the whole time. The secret to their success is in how they budget their time and priorities.

Create a Time Budget

Our money is valuable to us, so we make sure to budget what we have to make it last. We often sit down and plan how we will spend our money based on how much we bring in. The concept is simple: If we overspend, we will struggle with debt. But if we are disciplined, we get to enjoy what money can offer. Our time is similar, and in some cases even more valuable. Try applying those money-budgeting principles to your allowance of time, and you'll find yourself cutting back on wasted time and investing wisely. You'll also achieve better balance. A time budget allows us to visualize exactly how much time we have on our hands, and helps us determine what we need to accomplish in that time to achieve balance.

Create Your Time Budget by Fixing Your Calendar

A fixed calendar is a calendar that schedules time in chunks. Many of us create a schedule based on how much time we need for a specific task or appointment, but a fixed calendar allows us to place those responsibilities and tasks into areas. This gives us more control over how our time is spent. In a financial budget, we create categories like home expenses, vacation fund, and groceries. We then allot a certain amount of money to each category.

When we treat our time that way, we can get a lot more done and find a better balance. "Chunk" your time into categories, and then put the tasks in the category in which they fit best. This gives you a plan for each day—a certain amount of time to spend on each category—and gives you the boundaries to make sure that you hit all categories, rather than leaving some of them unfinished.

Fix your calendar to include these three categories:

- **Sleep.** Designate the amount of time you want to sleep. Eight to ten hours of sleep a night means you are well rested and able to perform better for your students. It will also give you the energy you need throughout the day. Sleep is crucial for success and balance.

- **Personal/me time.** Designate time for family, friends, or yourself. This time gives you a chance to unwind from your workday, and allows you to recharge. This looks different for everyone. Some people recharge by learning new things, while others need a full escape from school and learning. What you do during your personal time is up to you, but the goal is to relax and unwind. If you enter your classroom refreshed each day, you will be a more effective teacher and a happier person.

- **Work/school.** Designate the amount of time you will spend on school-related tasks during the week. Utilize work time for work. Spend your time collaborating with colleagues, planning lessons, and assessing students, and dedicate some of your school time to accomplishing these tasks. That way you cut back on work tasks once you leave the classroom. Make it a goal to never bring work home with you.

When creating your fixed calendar, feel free to add additional sections that address important things in your life. You may have more than three categories, but the key is to lay it out ahead of time so you always know what your schedule will be. When you use a fixed calendar and you find a format that works, you will have essentially the same schedule every single week. (For example, in my fixed calendar, I dedicate my Saturdays to family, and don't leave any room for work. This allows me to plan ahead because I already know what all of my Saturdays look like.)

Of course, you should also leave space in your time budget for "fun money." Fun money is the money designated for things we enjoy, such as going out to dinner, going to the movies, or even setting money aside for personal shopping. This flexibility is also crucial in your time budget. Set aside time to do what you love, and choose a day each week for that chunk of time. We have to explore the things we love if we're to be the best versions of ourselves—both inside and outside the classroom. Schedule something to look forward to, and you'll find that it gets you through the tough days. Your experiences during that time will also spill over into your classroom and benefit your students, as well.

Two Things to Consider When Budgeting Your Work Time

- **Get in the flow.** It takes approximately fifteen minutes of uninterrupted time to become fully focused and engaged with a task. Keep that as your goal, and dedicate an appropriate amount of time in your time budget to each task, to make sure you can work without distraction. Start each session by eliminating the desire to multitask. This is time dedicated to *one thing*. The goal is to avoid surfing the internet, using social media, or text messaging (anything other than an emergency should be ignored) so that you can focus on the task at hand. Once you are in the flow, you may find that you are more productive than ever before.

- **Chunk your planning.** Planning lessons can take a long time. Chunk your days when you are planning, and focus on one plan per day. If you teach multiple subjects, designate a day for each subject (for example, Monday: Math; Tuesday: Science). Try to keep a week ahead in your planning so you don't have to do all the plans in one day. Using your weekdays to plan this way can free up your weekends for more personal time, giving you better balance, and allowing you to have the energy to become an uNforgettable teacher.

Sign a Boundary Contract

Finding balance is not only about time. We might budget our time perfectly ... and still find that there aren't enough hours in the day to complete everything we have to do. Becoming overwhelmed and stressed about a lack of time is not the way to become an uNforgettable teacher. Instead, you'll be going through the motions and treating your students as afterthoughts. So how do we avoid the problem?

Many of us have trouble saying no because it is in our nature to help others. We end up taking on more than we can handle, which causes stress and resentment. Instead of teaching, which we love, we get busy doing favors that we never wanted to do. Our life begins to spiral out of control—all because we never set boundaries, and therefore we said yes to too many things. Ultimately, our passion takes a back seat to stress—and our students notice.

Combat this problem by creating a contract with yourself. When we sign a teaching contract, we are saying we will abide by what's in it, and meet the expectations we've just signed on for. If we do not follow through with that, we can be fired or sued. They are powerful pieces of paper that bring joy to those who receive them and pain to those who break them. The same concept works with a boundary contract. This contract is one you design and outlines what you're willing to take on outside of your normal teaching responsibilities—and what you are not.

Here are some examples. If you enjoy heading up committees to help develop the school, include it in the contract as one of your outside activities. If you do not, include it in the contract as a responsibility that is not acceptable to you. If you are willing to take on a coaching responsibility or an after-school club, include it in the contract. If not, make sure to list that as something you are not willing to take on during the year. Put these things down in writing and then sign it, and you'll have a document to review down the line when you're faced with a decision. Making that decision, and avoiding the overwhelm that comes with overpromising, will help you achieve better balance.

Elements of Your Boundary Contract

- **The offer.** This is a constant reminder of the reward you're going to give yourself for having the courage to say no. Your offer may sound something like: "By only saying yes to tasks I am passionate about, and taking on tasks I want to do rather than things I feel obligated to do, I will gain time to do the activities of my choice."

- The **agreement.** This is the section that contains what you are willing to do and what you are not willing to do. Create a list of reasonable tasks you will take on, or the amount of time you are willing to put in outside of teaching. Think of activities that you are passionate about and that will help your students succeed. Time is precious, so this should only include activities and options that will help your students shine, or will help your passion spread. Moving forward, don't agree to any tasks that don't fit those categories.

- The **consideration.** This is the section where you explain the promise and set a time period. You can create a contract with yourself for a month, a couple of months, or even the entire year. Place an endpoint to the contract so you can look back, reflect, and renegotiate if needed, once you've realized that part of the contract doesn't work the way you thought it would.

Follow the Rule of Threes

People remember things when they are in threes. Great presentations are usually broken down into three main points. Plays are divided into three acts. Even the military breaks tasks into chunks of three for soldiers. The reason is simply that three is easier to remember than higher numbers.

Implement the Rule of Threes to help you find balance. When you have a handle on time and boundaries, you may be tempted to do more simply because you have the time to do so. The Rule of Threes will keep you from spiraling back into an unbalanced lifestyle. Here's how to use the Rule of Threes to help you find balance:

- **Set three goals.** At the start of each day, set three main goals for the day. These goals should be reasonable, measurable, and attainable. Write these goals down and make sure they are visible or with you throughout the day, so you can mark them off once they are done.

- **Complete the goals.** When you've completed all three goals, rest. Do not attempt to take on more tasks or responsibilities for the day. The reason you have three goals is so that you can accomplish them and plan to meet three more the next day. Doing more than you have to will eventually lead to stress and unbalance.

- **Goals left undone.** If the day passes and you are not able to complete all three goals, simply shift the unfinished goals to the next day. Do not add them to the next set of goals you have listed. Give each day only three goals to avoid becoming overwhelmed.

- **Celebrate your day.** When you complete your three goals for the day, give yourself time to celebrate. Take time for yourself or spend time with family and friends. You may not accomplish your three goals every day, and that is OK. Over time, you will find that your celebrations are becoming more frequent—and that you're getting more done.

uNleash Your Newfound Freedom

Students remember a teacher who is on fire more than one who is burned out. When we find balance, we become happier in our personal lives, our teaching improves, and our students reap the benefits. When we learn to manage our energy and budget our time, we open a whole world of possibilities to become uNforgettable. We find small moments to spend listening to students and learning more about who they are as people. Setting boundaries means we set ourselves free from the grip of obligation and instead enjoy teaching with passion. Finding balance in our lives will benefit everyone we come into contact with, and by implementing a few strategies, we can change our lives for the better.

- **Reflect.** Balance in your life will impact your students in many ways. They will see a happier and more confident you, and will experience the best you have to offer. Think about these simple questions as you reflect on your work-life balance:

- How much time do you spend thinking about work compared to the time you concentrate on other things you enjoy?

- What do you need to do in order to find a work-life balance?

- **uNleash.** Choose one new action to do today. In order to find balance in your life, you need to actively pursue it. Finding that balance will lead to a happier life, and you'll be able to spread joy to those around you. Instead of sitting and complaining, though, you have to take the steps to get it done. The following actions will help you begin finding balance in your life. Write down one that you are ready to uNleash this week, and commit to carrying it out:

  - Create and sign your boundary contract.

  - Fix your calendar to focus on the three areas in the Time Budget section of this chapter.

  - Set your three goals for today and begin making it a habit.

- **Get social.** Take a picture of your fixed calendar or boundary contract and share it to inspire others. Post your picture on social media using the hashtag #WeTeachuN.

Lean on Others

If everyone is moving forward together, then success takes care of itself. — HENRY FORD

Destination Guide Seven
....

WHEN IT COMES
TO OUR TEACHING,
WE WANT TO FIND
PEOPLE WHO HAVE
OUR BEST INTERESTS,
AND OUR STUDENTS'
BEST INTERESTS,
AT HEART.

uNveil Your Strength

WE ARE STRONGER together.

Superheroes in movies never succeed alone. The Justice League, for example, is a powerful team of superheroes comprised of some of the most recognizable faces of all time, such as Wonder Woman, Batman, and Superman, to name a few. Alone, each hero is powerful, yet together they are an unstoppable force to be reckoned with. As a teacher, you bring your own unique skill set into the profession—your own superpowers. Alone, you are powerful, but imagine if we attempt to "save the world" together instead of going at it alone. Just like the Justice League, when we work together, we can change the world. When we share our strengths, we become uNforgettable. Teaching is not about being in competition with one another, but rather collaboration. The ultimate goal is to use our strengths to collectively inspire and prepare our students for the future.

uNforgettable teachers want to be part of, or create, their own Justice League. They understand that our greatest resource is each other, and that standing alone often keeps us from moving forward.

Teaching can sometimes feel like an enigma. In one moment we feel like we have everything under control, while in the next it seems that our whole class is falling apart. When we try to figure out every issue by ourselves or attempt to personally analyze why something went wrong, we often lose the balance we so diligently worked to achieve. This is when we need one another the most. We build community in our classrooms and form a family bond with our students. Imagine what could happen if we did the same thing with our colleagues.

If we learn to lean on each other during our times of need and our times of triumph, we build a culture within our building and community that focuses on the strengths that bind us. We become a family of people willing to help each other through struggles and come together to form a team of teaching superheroes. When we collaborate with those around us and lean on each other, we become better. We become uNforgettable.

Leaning on Others Requires Trust

Do you trust the people you're around every day? Trust is the foundation that allows us to lean on each other without fear. Imagine yourself hanging over a cliff, grasping onto a rope for dear life, with only one person holding the other end of that rope. Your only hope for survival lies in that person's hands. Who would you trust in that position?

The people you name should make up your teaching team. A team is only as strong as its weakest link, and when you make a team, you want to feel you can trust each member. Leaning on a group of people you trust allows you to stop trying to solve problems on your own. Instead, the team will tackle tough problems together in order to give students the best experience possible. We often think of uNforgettable teachers as individuals who stand out from the crowd, but in reality, the most memorable teachers are those who have a powerful force of trusted colleagues behind them. Collaboration and constructive criticism form the basis of becoming uNforgettable, and trust is the foundation. Teachers rarely leave a lasting impression by doing everything on their own.

The truth is, though, that not everyone we work with is someone we want on our team. We need to take the time to find the people we trust. A strong team member remains steadfast when we need them the most. A weak one falters and breaks. When it comes to our teaching, we want to find people who have our best interests, and our students' best interests, at heart. We want to find colleagues who will challenge us and push us to be better, and who strive for excellence in and out of the classroom. This relationship is not only about supporting each other, but also about growing.

Leaning on Others Provides Innovation

Once you find your team, you'll start to reap amazing benefits. Brainstorming together and sharing lesson ideas with others gives you the chance to look at problems in an entirely new way. A team also ensures that you have someone supporting you, which means you'll have more confidence to try new things and take risks. Having a trusted team of colleagues to lean on will give you the platform you need to bring about innovation.

Combine that innovation (or the ability to get things done) with creativity (or the spark of new ideas)—and you'll create an entirely new classroom experience. You'll be even more successful if you continue to lean on others to help you initiate those new ideas.

We can take our material and turn it into something fun and amazing, but there is only so much we can do on our own. Use your team for feedback and brainstorming as you come up with new ideas and ways to implement them. Sharing these ideas and planning sessions helps everyone grow, and strengthens the entire team, and when you have an idea that you can't execute on your own, you'll be able to call on your team for help. When we lean on each other and share our ideas, we break open the doors to our classrooms and let our creativity spill out into the hallways, leaving an uNforgettable imprint.

uNravel a Plan to Create an Inner Circle You Can Trust

When we refuse to lean on others and we take on everything alone, we end up isolated at the moment when we need help the most. We also isolate ourselves within the school community—and it is difficult to be uNforgettable to our students when we are forgotten by our peers. Our students notice everything that we do, and they pay attention to who we talk to and who we interact with daily. They notice when we are distant from our colleagues and when we refuse to ask for help. They often take cues on how to interact with their peers based on how we act around ours. We, therefore, have negative or positive impacts on our students, based on how we handle our own relationships. When we find people we can lean on, they bring out the best in everything we do, and our students have a terrific example to follow. The key is figuring out the difference between who we can trust and who we should keep at a friendly distance so that we present our students with the best possible examples.

Build an Inner Circle

Think of people you consider to be great leaders. They most likely have surrounded themselves with others who make (or made) them better. They understand that their characters are being built by the people who influence them every day. They have learned over time that their inner circle can help them either develop or regress, and they have chosen to surround themselves with people who have a positive effect.

Take a look around at the people you interact with most in your professional world. When you are in the faculty room, are they gossiping and bringing others down, or are they lifting people up? When you are looking to collaborate, do they inspire you and motivate you to be better, or are they watching the clock and counting the minutes until they can leave? Gossip and negativity will fill our school buildings and can lead us down a path that will inevitably end up in a place we don't want to be. Following that road, as tempting as it may be, will have repercussions that spill over into your classroom and your life. If you get caught up with those who enjoy gossip and thrive on negativity, you will become just like them.

It's up to you to make sure that doesn't happen.

Although we are surrounded by gossip and negativity as teachers, we don't have to be a part of it. We have the choice. Where there is gossip, you will also find those who stand up for the truth. Where there is negativity, you will always find a positive light shining through to break the darkness. When you choose positivity and surround yourself with people who stand up for the truth, you take the steps toward becoming an uNforgettable teacher, and your students will come back to visit again and again over the years.

IF YOU WANT TO MOVE FORWARD AS A TEACHER, YOU NEED TO FIGURE OUT WHETHER THE PEOPLE AROUND YOU ARE MOVING YOU FORWARD OR HOLDING YOU BACK.

How do you make sure you're choosing the right people? Consider your current inner circle and decide on the five people who influence you the most. They tend to be the ones who impact you on a daily basis—and impress your thoughts even more than you realize.

Find Your Top Five

If you want to move forward as a teacher, you need to figure out whether the people around you are moving you forward or holding you back. Next time you are with colleagues, take note of what you talk about. Does your conversation lead to an improvement in your teaching or in your life, or do you leave the conversations feeling bad about yourself? When you discuss what you are teaching, do they change the subject and steer it toward the latest gossip, or do they jump in to brainstorm with you in order to make your idea better?

Change your mindset, and start to look for people who will help you move forward. You don't have to end friendships, of course, but narrow your "professional" inner circle and find people who influence you to improve.

Think about the five people you're around most during the day in your professional life. Write down their names and make it a point to reach out and work together often. Try to set one day a week, if possible, to grab coffee and brainstorm together. It will pay dividends in the future and will help you continue to grow. Consider the five types of people you want to look for as you build that inner circle for the best possible success.

Five People You Want in Your Inner Circle

We come across so many different types of teachers during our school day. Some will inspire us with their creativity, while others will impress us with their ability to get everything done. We will notice the colleagues we get along with and the colleagues we don't particularly like. Our inner circle, however, is not a fan fest or popularity contest. It should be a community of educators who share the goal of helping students succeed, and who want to grow in their practice. It should be filled with imperfect people who think differently and challenge each other to become better.

An uNforgettable teacher cannot fit neatly into a box, so we don't need to fill our inner circles with people who all think the same. Surrounding ourselves only with people who think like us will not bring about new ideas or growth. When we have a mix of qualities filling our inner circle, we avoid a fixed mindset as we move forward. Instead, the different strengths and ideas bring about a complete brain trust of people who think in different ways, yet share the desire for growth. Building an inner circle filled with different strengths and opinions allows us to become comfortable being uncomfortable, and sometimes that is what we need for growth.

Start building your inner circle by looking at the qualities people possess. Here are five types of people you might want to include. Keep in mind that some people may hold more than one of these qualities—and that these aren't the only qualities to look for. This is just a starting point for your journey toward being uNforgettable.

- **The Mentor.** With experience comes wisdom. Try to connect with someone who has the experience and wisdom to help you overcome things you have never been through. You need to have someone who can keep you on track, inspire you with ideas that others do not see, and lend you a little brilliance once in a while. A mentor balances you out and gives you direction when you need it most.

- **The Logical Mind.** You also need someone who is logical and honest. Find someone who will tell it like it is without trying to sugarcoat everything. This is a person you can go to for advice when tough situations arise. The person's honesty is invaluable, if he or she has your best interest at heart.

- **The Innovator.** You need someone who is willing to push the boundaries every once in a while; a risk-taker who can take ideas and make them better, and inspire others by challenging them. Surround yourself with someone who challenges your thinking, and you'll grow quickly.

- **The Go-Getter.** This is a person who has no problem taking charge and getting things done, and is excited to do what is best for students. The go-getter follows through on commitments and excites us when we are lacking energy. Most important, this person is reliable. We all need someone we can count on to get the job done!

- **The True Friend.** You need someone in your inner circle who can hold things together when they go awry. This is the person you can trust no matter what, who will support you during the toughest of times. You can vent to this person without judgment, and trust him or her to keep things confidential when needed. True friendship is difficult to find, and without it in your inner circle, you might lose sight of who you are and where you're going.

The goal is to have a give-and-take relationship with your inner circle so that you're all growing together. If you find that one member isn't contributing much, it might mean they're wrong for your group. Never be a constant taker, and avoid those who are. This might be the person who uses the ideas and lessons shared in the group but never offers ideas or lessons to help bring improvement to others, or the one who takes all the credit for an idea, even though it came from others. Remember, ultimately it is about bringing excellence to the students we teach, and the people within your inner circle should all contribute to that goal.

Surround yourself with mentors, innovators, and other people you trust, and you will find yourself continually growing, learning, and changing the lives of students in ways they will never forget. When *you're* challenged to stretch and grow, you will be able to challenge your students to do the same.

Grow Your PLN and Add to Your Inner Circle

You don't have to confine your inner circle to your own school building, either. Although there are advantages to leaning on peers that you see each day, you'll reap benefits from virtual colleagues as well. In order to be uNforgettable in this world of technology, we must be willing to embrace every medium available to improve ourselves, and think beyond the classroom walls to impact our students, because empowered teachers empower teachers.

A PLN, or personal learning network, can consist of peers you see every day, as well as people from all over the world. Building a PLN is a crucial component to teaching forward— and it is important to building your inner circle and leaning on them for growth and expansion in your classroom.

Two Simple Ways to Build or Grow Your PLN

1. Get social.

Social media is a powerful tool when used properly. Teachers are sharing and brainstorming through Twitter, Facebook, Instagram, and more, in ways they've never been able to do before. They are challenging each other to be better and teach differently. Whether you are new to social media or a seasoned veteran, use it to help you in your own growth, utilizing these three tips:

- Follow education hashtags like #HackLearning, #JoyfulLeaders, #masterychat, #edchat, and #WeTeachuN, to name a few. Hashtags are often associated with chats that give you access to many educators looking for community. They are a perfect way to grow your PLN and meet like-minded educators.

- Read and reach. Share your favorite blog posts, podcasts, and articles often, and tag the authors of the pieces to let them know you enjoyed their work. Look for relevant content that has helped you or can help others in education. Reach out to the authors and begin a conversation with them. Most education bloggers, podcasters, and authors are happy to help you whenever they can.

- Use the 80/20 rule when posting on social media for educational purposes. This means that 80 percent of the content you share should be resources that have helped or inspired you, and 20 percent should be promoting you or your personal work. You can promote different ways of thinking and teaching by sharing your own work, and connect with people who want to know more about your theories. People want to be part of a PLN that encourages diverse thinking, and your ideas might start a conversation that leads to a lifelong friendship.

2. Nourish your roots.

It is easy to take the colleagues we teach with each day for granted. Never lose track of those in your own building, and how you can help each other. Although our online PLN can transform us into better teachers, a face-to-face conversation with a fellow teacher in our buildings can be just as powerful. We have a connection with our peers that just doesn't exist online because in many instances we teach the same kids. When we can build a personal learning network within our school, we can help each other grow, and meet the individual needs of the specific students we all teach. Here are two simple ways to build an in-building personal network:

- Plan together. We need to teach our students in ways that are fresh and new, and that becomes easier if we work together—particularly if we're trying to reach the same students. Plan together, bounce ideas around, and come up with paths that work for the group you're teaching.

- Critique each other. Nobody likes to be critiqued, but we grow when we receive honest feedback. Make weekly feedback sessions a part of your routine, and share ideas as often as possible. What works in one class may not work in another, so a feedback session can be a helpful way to share your strengths and ideas. When we allow ourselves to be vulnerable, we grow and embrace the changes we may need as we prepare for the future.

We do amazing things and have outstanding ideas that we implement in our classrooms. The problem is that we are often afraid to share anything, due to a fear of rejection. When we have an inner circle and a PLN we can lean on, we can be fearless, because we know we have people supporting us. Take the time to share what you do in your class. Share your materials with each other. Share your wins and your struggles. When you are willing to take a step out of your comfort zone and share your genius with others, you will improve, and your circle of trust will grow.

uNleash an Unbreakable Bond

Kids never forget the teachers who made them smile or helped them feel good about themselves, and colleagues will always remember the one who encouraged them. Be that person for them, and you will be uNforgettable. Take action and set the example to spread the trust to the entire building. We are much stronger together than we could ever be alone. When we are brave enough to lean on one another in our teaching, we will become more impactful and influential.

- **Reflect:** It can be difficult to find people we trust enough to lean on. Think about the people you currently have around you. Who are you around the most? Are you able to lean on them when you need to? Are they helping you grow as a teacher?

- **uNleash:** Evaluate your inner circle and take action! Decide how you feel about those in your inner circle, and whether they're doing what you need them to do. These should be the people who encourage us when we need it, and celebrate with us when we succeed. The following two actions will help you start to build an inner circle in your professional life. Write down one action that you are ready to uNleash this week, and commit to carrying it out.

  - Review the section titled, "Five People You Want in Your Inner Circle" from this chapter and create a list of people who fit each quality. Decide which of them you would like in your inner circle and reach out to them.

  - Build your PLN. If you aren't on social media for teaching, start today. Sign up for Twitter and search for some great educators. If you want to connect with me, you can find me @cpoole27. Say hello and let me know who you are, because I would love to be a part of your online PLN!

- **Get social:** Post a picture or give a shout-out to someone you consider to be in your inner circle, and thank the person for what he or she brings to your life. Share on social media using the hashtag #WeTeachuN.

Teach Forward

The people who are crazy enough to think they can change the world are the ones who do. — STEVE JOBS

Destination Guide Eight

DESTINATION EIGHT

TEACHING FORWARD AND ADAPTING TO OUR CURRENT WORLD MEANS MORE THAN SIMPLY IMPLEMENTING TECHNOLOGY OR FOLLOWING THE LATEST TRENDS, ALTHOUGH THESE ARE IMPORTANT. IT IS ABOUT GROWING IN OUR TEACHING STYLES, TO TAKE NOT ONLY NEW TECHNOLOGY INTO ACCOUNT, BUT OUR STUDENTS AS WELL.

uNveil Change and Growth

YOU ARE AN arborist who fills the world with growing trees.

In our world, we cannot exist without trees. They are an essential part of the lifeblood that allows Earth to function. As the biggest plants on the planet, they give us oxygen, store carbon, stabilize the soil, and make energy. Without trees, we would not be able to survive. In many ways, our students are like trees—which makes uNforgettable teachers like arborists. We can nourish and protect them so that they can grow and become part of the lifeline of the future.

Roots are the strength of trees. The stronger the roots, the more powerful and healthy the trees. As they grow, they will bask in the sunlight and get battered by storms. Their leaves will change color and display beauty, and possibly fall and wither for a season. Their roots keep them grounded and strong through every triumph and obstacle. Our students also need a firm, predictable foundation, and as the arborists, we must help them achieve it. This means keeping up with the changes in our world—including technological advances and innovation—so that we can teach them forward, and prepare them for the future.

With every student we care for and educate, we offer a gift to the future. The next great innovator, doctor, scientist, and teacher may be sitting in our classrooms right now. But they're moving into a future and a world that is different from the one in which we grew up, and we must teach them in the way that best suits that future. Just as arborists have the vision of what a tree will become when they plant a tiny seed into the soil, uNforgettable teachers guide their students with the vision of what they will become in the future. Teaching forward means looking at the big picture, seeing where our students are headed, and based on that vision, paving a pathway they can follow toward success.

Teaching Forward Encourages Change

The trees that we see in our world all began as small seeds. Although they bloom into different species, they all have one thing in common: They all change over time. They go from small seeds to saplings to wonderful and powerful trees. That sort of change occurs constantly in our world, and the same is true of human society. Much of the technology we have today will be obsolete within a few months, and strategies that we are told to try are often replaced with new ones within a few years.

Change can be a beautiful thing, depending on your outlook. When it comes to teaching students, the changing technology creates a world of new opportunities. That means we need to change how we teach to better suit their needs and their futures. Our students are living in a world that is foreign to us in so many ways. They face information overload on a daily basis and have the answers to their questions available to them within seconds of searching.

Teaching with a forward-thinking mindset means being open to all of that, and being more interested in having our students think for themselves, rather than asking them something they can figure out with a quick internet search. Instead of giving information, we need to provide wisdom and sharpen their skills. We need to teach them to think critically and solve problems. We're helping them develop roots of good citizenship, trustworthiness, respect, responsibility, and fairness. To do that, we have to think bigger and progress into the future.

Teaching forward and adapting to our current world means more than simply implementing technology or following the latest trends, although these are important. It is about growing in our teaching styles, to take not only new technology into account, but our students as well. When the way we always taught something stops yielding success, it means it's time to find a new strategy. Teaching forward means being open to that possibility, and taking advantage of it when it presents itself.

We are helping to raise the leaders of tomorrow, and we are partly responsible for their development. When we model for them what it means to be a good person, to serve others, and to demonstrate empathy, we encourage a more responsible future. When we teach them to think critically, we prepare them to overcome obstacles in their paths. When we show them how to collaborate and work together, even when they don't like the people they are working with, we prepare them for the real world. All of these things move them forward, and when they are combined with the content we cover, our class can become uNforgettable.

When you can relate what they are learning to their world, and show them how the skills you are teaching will benefit them in their future, they will become engaged. And they will remember the teacher who showed them the path forward, and how to walk it successfully.

Teaching Forward Empowers Growth

A tree does not become strong and healthy overnight but rather needs help from Mother Nature (or a gardener) so it can thrive. Our students also grow gradually in their learning, and each one will go at his or her own pace. Some need more "watering" than others, but they will all grow when they have a caring teacher by their sides. When we commit to teaching forward, we become the guides they need as they walk through their many stages of learning. We become their lifelines, their confidence-builders, and the ones they lean on in their times of need. We give them the tools they need if they're to survive in a world that is constantly changing.

So how do we encourage that growth? We live in a fast-paced world filled with people who are always in a hurry. But to move forward, we need to slow down and embrace the moment. This isn't easy because society tells us to move without slowing down, and makes us believe that the world will pass us by if we let it. Although there is some truth to this sentiment, a major component of growth is having the ability to learn from the past, be present in the moment, and adjust when needed to prepare for the future. If our students feel that they have to run as quickly as they can at all times, we have set them up for failure rather than growth.

To truly grow into a powerful future citizen, students must also know how to slow down and reflect. As forward-thinking teachers, we need to show them how to do this. When students do not understand something in the moment, take the time to re-teach them a concept before moving forward. Teach them to stop their movement and allow their brains to work and solve the problem. If they have had success with a concept in the past, allow them to pause and help others who may be falling behind. Utilize the guidance in this book about taking the time to set up a classroom atmosphere that is grounded in relationships, encourages student ownership, and embraces failure. Doing so empowers the students and teaches them to move forward at their own pace, rather than a pace that is forced upon them.

This shows them that their learning is more important than simply getting through a lesson, and they will come to value understanding and growth over speed. We must foster a culture of people who are willing to slow down and adapt to change so that they can transition with the world and continue to grow as it alters around them. They will collaborate with each other, think for themselves, and rise to the challenges they face because we taught them to do so, and gave them a place to learn how.

Teaching forward is a nebulous theory and there are so many ways to do it that the options can become overwhelming. Follow these simple strategies so you can start teaching forward right away.

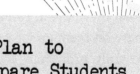

uNravel a Plan to Prepare Students for Tomorrow

Teach Forward Through Engagement

Military generals would never go into battle without a detailed plan. They would account for every minute of movement and put backup plans in place in order to carry out their missions successfully. If something in the plan changes, the best generals are able to adapt. As teachers, we can engage our students in the same way by planning our "missions" carefully and learning to adapt to their needs—or teaching forward. When our students are engaged in their learning, they will find ways to break the barriers they often believe are in their way, and will learn to be more self-sufficient. uNforgettable teachers embrace the way modern students learn and find ways to let them create experiences that are relevant to them. The results may surprise you.

Let Them Create

Every student we teach is filled with brilliance just waiting to be uNleashed. When we give them the opportunity to demonstrate it, amazing things can happen. We are heading toward a future that will require independent people who can think critically and creatively based on new ideas.

uNforgettable teachers teach forward by handing over the reins from time to time and allowing students the chance to demonstrate their brilliance in relevant ways. Use the following tips to let them get creative and show you what they can do.

Create a Class YouTube Channel or Class Podcast

Throughout the year, the main way our students demonstrate their learning is through written tests. We grade them based on their performance, and the class moves on to the next lesson. Students who do poorly on a test may label themselves as people who can't succeed, and then head down the wrong path.

But that path could have been different. Imagine if those students were able to harness the knowledge and be assessed not by a grade, but rather by a demonstration of their knowledge in action.

ONCE THEY CREATE A VIDEO THAT GOES LIVE OR A PODCAST THAT IS ON THE AIRWAVES, THEY CAN START TO SEE THE VALUE IN THEIR LEARNING. THEY WILL SEE THEIR OWN BRILLIANCE IN ACTION, AND WILL HAVE CONNECTED THEIR LEARNING TO SOMETHING IN THE REAL WORLD.

A class YouTube channel or a class podcast are the perfect platforms for allowing students to demonstrate what they have learned and share it with the world. For example, creating a video series on how an ancient culture affects our world today would demonstrate more insight and relevance than a test that requires memorized answers. It would show them that their knowledge is important and interesting to people around the world, and offer them a valid way of demonstrating what they have learned. They might also gain a deeper understanding about a topic you've covered in class by doing an audio interview with an expert (in many cases, one of their teachers). Once they create a video that goes live or a podcast that is on the airwaves, they can start to see the value in their learning. They will see their own brilliance in action, and will have connected their learning to something in the real world. For teachers, this will be a brand new and exciting way to assess their knowledge. And a class where students are encouraged to break the mold in this way quickly becomes a class that they will never forget.

Ideas for a Class YouTube Channel or Podcast

Create a How-To channel or podcast, where students demonstrate how to do the things they learned in class. It could be a how-to video on writing essays, performing lab experiments, or even how to do math problems. It could be short podcast episodes explaining one concept at a time. The key is to give them the freedom to explore and demonstrate to the world what they have learned.

Create an Ask the Student Channel or Podcast. Plan for students to answer questions that are common during specific units of study. Provide them with the questions and give them time to come up with the answers. You will find that students can explain concepts to their peers more effectively than we ever could.

Create a Class Video Blog (vlog). Encourage students to vlog about what they are learning in class or their experiences in school. Their messages might open our eyes to what they need.

Create an Interview-Based Podcast. Schedule time with other teachers in the building, the principal, or any staff, and let students ask them relevant questions. This can give teachers an opportunity to build relationships with their students outside of the classroom, and will give students a chance to delve deeper into concepts with their teachers.

Create Innovative Thinking

The future will be filled with entrepreneurs who will shape our world with their creativity and ideas, and those entrepreneurs might be sitting in your class right now. To get them on the right path, we must nourish and celebrate their skills and talents, and be forward-thinking enough to recognize their brilliance. Teach forward by creating simple challenges that show them the value of hard work and determination—to spark their creativity and get them thinking for themselves.

Types of Challenges to Spark Innovation

- **The product challenge.** Implement an Innovation Friday where you set up a challenge and inspire students to come up with the best ideas. Give them an everyday product to focus on, and ask them to make it better. Allow them two minutes to sell their idea through an elevator pitch, and then determine a winner.

- **The lesson challenge.** We often teach concepts that our students find difficult to grasp. Create concept cards with topics they have learned in the past. Pass them out and have the students think of new ways to teach those concepts, then have them present the new teaching unit to the class.

- **The business challenge.** Have students turn a concept that you have taught them into a business. Let them create the plan for what the business would look like, how they would make money, and who their customers would be. Give them time to pitch the idea in a Shark Tank type of setting, and then determine who you would invest in.

Giving our students a chance to create things based on what they know will engage them and give them an experience they will remember. It will teach them critical thinking skills and give them problem-solving opportunities that they will need in the future. When we teach our students to innovate and allow them to embrace failure along the way, they will grow and succeed.

Imagine if students walked into our classrooms and stepped into experiences they would remember forever. Innovative teachers remain in the minds of students forever, because they are often the ones who inspire the biggest experiences and ideas.

Teach Forward Through Empathy

Creativity and innovation are two key elements of teaching forward, and empathy is a third. Our students must learn empathy and take it with them as they grow, so they can understand and share the feelings of others. When we teach empathy, we prepare our students for successful interactions with their fellow citizens. If we are diligent in showing them the benefits of a caring heart, our society as a whole will be better off in the years to come.

One of the biggest challenges in teaching empathy, however, is time. It isn't easy to plan in lessons that fully encompass this topic, so the most effective way is to implement it through daily and weekly routines that take little to no class time at all. Try one of these simple ideas to get started.

Set the Example and Lead with Love

In our classrooms, we often use graphic organizers, tech tools, and other methods to guide our students in their tasks. Teach empathy in a similar manner. Demonstrate how to take the feelings of other people into consideration and treat them with kindness, and it gives your students a template to follow. Sometimes all they need to see is the lesson in action.

Pay It Forward

Our students love challenges. When we give them a goal to accomplish, the outcomes can be remarkable. To teach empathy in a way that gives students power, create Pay It Forward challenges. You will transform the culture in your classroom—and perhaps in the school itself.

A few ways to hold Pay It Forward challenges:

- **Create a weekly kindness-themed challenge.** Each week, post a theme for students to focus on. Themes can range from "Write a positive note to a teacher or friend" to "Open the door for someone." Some will be simple, and some will be complex, yet they will all change your students' mindsets. Create a goal of finding out how much kindness your class can spread throughout the year. Track these random acts by asking students to report when they are on the receiving end rather than the giving end. Create a Kindness Wall to track the results visually.

- **Get one, give one challenge.** Model what you mean by writing personal notes of encouragement to different students every week or two. When you give out a note, share a blank one as well, and ask them to write a note for someone else. Create a sentence stem for them to use, or create notes with inspirational quotes on one side and blank pages on the other. Model what a kind word of encouragement looks like, then allow them to follow in your footsteps and pay it forward.

Create an Emotion Daily Roadmap

Use this same model in journal form for the students themselves. Create a template for students to fill out every day, whether written in a journal or placed in a planner. The goal is to help them identify their emotions for specific events. Set it up with three sections:

- **Section One: Set the destination.** Students list what they expect to encounter that day that will be a disruption of some sort. This could range from a big test to a presentation, or an after-school activity.

- **Section Two: Identify the emotion.** Students list what they're feeling about the destination they listed. For example, if they are going to perform in the play after school, they may feel nervous or afraid.

- **Section Three: Decide which path to take.** Students provide three possible paths they can take to help navigate the emotion that comes with the destination.

Destination	Emotion	Paths
Language Arts Presentation	Nervous, afraid, worried that I am not prepared	1. Practice presentation with a friend. 2. Create a note card to use while presenting. 3. Review presentation to make sure everything is covered.

Example of an Emotion Roadmap.

Teaching forward is about educating the entire student, and that includes teaching how to identify and handle emotions. When we focus on helping them develop their hearts as well as their minds, we prepare them for a successful future and an uNforgettable life.

uNleash the Foundation

One of the most powerful ways to teach forward is to invest. When we invest in our own learning, we change and grow. When we invest the time to teach students in ways they understand, and find strategies that are relevant to their world, we make an impact that will last for years. Our students deserve our best, and sometimes our most amazing ideas stem from the influences that surround us. These may be people we teach every day, the colleagues we interact with, or our social influences. Embrace the world as it changes, stay true to your roots, and work together to prepare your students for the future, and you will be a teacher who is teaching forward.

- **Reflect.** There are so many ways to engage and empower students. Sometimes we get caught up in what is easy, rather than what would really help our students grow. Reflect on the following questions to determine where you can improve in this aspect. In what ways do you empower your students to be the best they can be? What do you do each week to make sure you are teaching forward?

- **uNleash.** Teach forward today by choosing one of the following methods and going for it! Teaching forward means empowering your students to grow. Sometimes you will need to pause in the moment or reflect on the past in order to help them move forward. Other times you will be able to empower them to move at their own pace into the future. Take action today and choose to start with engagement or empathy as you implement a teaching-forward mentality in your classroom. Write down one of the following that you are ready to uNleash this week, and commit to carrying it out:

- Choose one way you will empower your students through engagement, using one of the strategies from the "Teach Forward Through Engagement" section to inspire you and get you started.

- Choose one way you will empower your students through empathy, using one of the strategies in the "Teach Forward Through Empathy" section.

- **Get social.** Send a shout-out to your "Top Ten" teachers in your PLN, and tell them how you see them teaching forward, using the hashtag #WeTeachuN.

Make Content Contagious

If you don't love what you do, you won't do it with much conviction or passion. — MIA HAMM

Destination Guide Nine

STUDENTS FALL IN
LOVE WITH CONTENT
THAT TEACHERS
LOVE TO TEACH.

uNveil the Biggest Fan

S TUDENTS FALL IN love with content that teachers love
to teach.

If you have ever been to professional baseball,
basketball, or soccer games, you have seen the team mascots. They are dressed up in costumes and interacting
with the audience in silly ways, or leading the charge to
support the teams. They are clearly passionate about who
they support. Their ultimate goal, however, is to make
sure that the fans have a good time and are the center of
attention. Their job is to energize the crowd and create an
atmosphere so contagious that everyone present wants
to be a part of the team "family."

As teachers, we must treat the content we teach like
the team we're endorsing. When we allow our passion for
what we teach to leak out, and we become the biggest
fans of our content—when we, in short, become our own
mascots—our subject matter becomes contagious. There
will be times when we interact in silly ways, and other
times when we lead the charge, but our ultimate goal is
to inspire our students to take things to a whole new level
on their own. The key is to show them that what they are
learning is relevant, and that it's OK to love every moment
of it. Those who love math, language arts, science, history, or any other subject usually love it because a past
teacher made it come alive for them. They often explore

specific topics because a teacher made it so interesting, exciting, or relevant that it became contagious.

Throughout this book, I have discussed the intangible qualities that help us find our ways into the hearts of students. I have covered some of the most important aspects of becoming a teacher they never forget. However, one crucial area that cannot be overlooked is the actual content we teach and how we teach it. When our students come into our classrooms, they know what subjects they will be learning. We must make it memorable, and make sure they hold onto it for years to come.

Making Content Contagious Sparks Curiosity

When we go to movie theaters, we know to expect about thirty minutes of previews for other movies before we get to see the one we came to watch. Film producers have figured out the secret to selling tickets: curiosity. They present quick glimpses of their upcoming movies to tease us. They don't need to give us all the information right away because they know that our curiosity will be enough to get us to the theater when a new film opens.

Teachers can follow that example. If we let our enthusiasm shine, our students will become those curious movie-goers who can't wait to see what our next classes will be about. How we demonstrate our passions might change depending on who we are as individuals. Some of us may dress up as a character when we teach a novel, or pose as a figure in history when we are studying a specific time period. We may bring personal connections into our content to show how it excites us in real life. We may form clubs and set up extra activities around the content for students to join in the fun.

The possibilities are endless, but when our students experience our content through the lens of our passions, they will start to realize how powerful the content can be. It gives them a glimpse of who we are outside of the classroom, and shows them that what we teach is part of who we are, and that we love it. They'll also become curious to learn more. We are essentially the movie preview for what we teach, and the more we demonstrate how passionate we are for our content, the more curious they will become.

Making Content Contagious Provides Authority

Curiosity often leads to exploration and a longing to go beyond the curriculum. Many of our students will take that curious spirit and go looking for a mentor to take them further than they could go alone. Some of the greatest mentors are those who are experts on subjects we find fascinating. We run to them when we have questions about their areas of expertise, and they make it evident through their actions that they love what they do. These mentors have proven time and again that they have the knowledge we seek, but also display passion and an undying desire to continue learning. It is that passion that keeps people coming back for more.

Our students look to us to be the authorities in what we

teach. If we simply go through the motions and lack energy, they will doubt our knowledge. If we offer them curriculum without insight, they will tune us out. But if we show our passions, and demonstrate how much we love what we teach, they'll treat us as authorities on the matter. They'll join in with our enthusiasm and come to us with any questions they can think up. We might not always know the answers, but they'll trust us to figure them out. Our enthusiasm will become their enthusiasm, and they will take more ownership of the subject—and start to make it relevant to their own lives.

When a great movie has an opening night, it sells out, and will probably continue to sell out in the weeks that follow. The process starts with the previews, but the word of mouth and contagious excitement truly make the magic happen. People begin stirring up excitement on their own, based on what they have seen already, and get others to join in on the fun. Teaching works the same way: Our passion provides a preview that sparks curiosity in our students and begins a buzz in the classroom. The students begin to talk among themselves, and before you know it, our content has become contagious with multiple students wanting to get involved.

uNravel a Plan to Make Your Content Contagious

Great leaders have a contagious attitude that sparks curiosity and makes others want to follow them no matter where they go. Our students are looking for people to lead them, and we can take advantage of that by becoming the authorities on subjects they find fascinating. uNforgettable teachers find ways to ignite curiosity in students, and then lead them into deeper explorations of the content in front of them. When a student comes into your class excited to learn, and leaves it with a desire to know more, you will become their natural leader. Meet with them individually to nurture that curiosity, and show them what else they can learn. Inspire them to work harder and learn more. Doing so will keep them on the edge of their seats, just waiting to learn more.

So how do you make sure your content is contagious to your students? The following few simple ideas will help you spark the fire. The key is to incorporate small ways for students to take ownership of the lessons they're learning.

Create an Inspiration Wall

Some teachers are uNforgettable because they are inspirational. They inspire their students to accomplish the unthinkable and help them rise to expectations they never thought they could reach. They instill a love of learning by making their content relevant to students in the real world. They teach students to share in the learning just like they share content online. Students are constantly influenced by what they interact with every day. They are sharing online, looking for approval from audiences, and finding the latest trends to join. Their sole focus on what they share and what they "like" revolves around them being the center of attention. They want to feel important and they want to feel as though other people think they are important. If we break into that world with a bit of our own content and show them how they can be the center of it all, we can become part of what they view as important. Half the battle of making our content contagious is getting it in front of those we teach in such a way that makes it a priority. A simple way to pique their interest is with an inspiration wall.

WHEN STUDENTS SEE THEIR WISDOM BEING RECOGNIZED, OTHERS WILL WANT TO JOIN IN, AND SHARING THEIR KNOWLEDGE ABOUT THE SUBJECT WILL SOON BECOME CONTAGIOUS.

An inspiration wall is a space set aside in the classroom to display student findings, successes, and positivity around your subject area, and it puts students at the center of it all. It motivates them by offering the chance to be recognized as someone who matters.

Three Simple Ways to Use the Inspiration Wall

1. Use the wall as a teaching tool. Our students say the craziest things. Sometimes they make us laugh, while other times they come up with wisdom beyond their years to inspire those

around them. Many students display their under-standing through what they say. We can use the inspiration wall to turn the positive comments they share into quotations.

When students share insightful comments pertaining to a lesson, write them down and place the "quotes" on the wall for all to see. Include the students' names and the dates so they will be given credit for their contributions. When students see their wisdom being recog-nized, others will want to join in, and sharing their knowledge about the subject will soon become contagious.

2. Use the wall as validation. Students always want to know how the learning will help them in life. One way to show them is to display how your content has made a difference in the world, or how it will help them in the future. Create a theme on your inspiration wall, and either keep it the same or change it every month, but make sure it relates to how your content affects the real world. Use "Famous People in Math History," "Amazing Scientific Discoveries that Changed Our World," or anything that relates to the sub-ject. Encourage students to find ideas to add to the wall, so that they're growing as learners while taking some ownership of the wall. This can spark inspiration inside of them and lead them down paths that will change their lives.

3. Personalize the wall for your students. Encourage them to find ways to demonstrate how *they* use the content you teach. Ask them to submit examples to place on the wall. By making it personal to them, you offer them the chance to demonstrate how valuable your content is in their lives. When students start sharing how the content impacts everyone around them, other students will follow, and the need to find new ways to show the content in action will become contagious.

The key to the inspiration wall is to make sure it is interactive rather than simply a bulletin board used for display. If we want our content to become contagious, we need to inspire students to love interacting with it consistently. Ask them to help you build the wall so it gains value in their eyes. Ask them to share their thoughts on topics related to your content by posting on the wall, and you'll eventually be able to use it as a point of reference. When they can see the value in what they're learning, they will raise the bar and begin to take that curiosity beyond the classroom walls.

Make Your Content Like a Brand

The most successful brands are contagious. People become fans of the brand and then start to spread the word on their own. Teachers need to brand their content so that their students do the same. Once you've established strong relationships with your students, they will love coming to class, and the next step is to connect your content to the environment you've formed in your classroom. Create assignments and experiences that include their interests, get to know what they want in their learning and give it to them. Feed their desire to be in your class, and you will get them fascinated in your content—and therefore your brand. The next section expands on these ideas in order to help you brand your content so your students equate the subject you teach with topics they love to learn.

Three Ways to Brand Your Content

Create desire.

A good brand gives people what they want. It provides quality and value that stand out above the rest. When a brand displays those benefits, it creates a desire for it. It might use humor or pull on the heartstrings, but it always offers people something of benefit.

Your students want to be part of something that will help them in the future. Show them how your content stands out and benefits them, and they will want to learn more. Pique their interest and be the teacher they can't wait to see, and you will draw them in. This doesn't mean that you become their best friend. It means that you are real with them, and vulnerable from time to time. When you are having a bad day, let them know instead of taking it out on them through your actions. When you are excited about something, share it with them. Tell them stories about your life that pertain to what you teach, and share events that demonstrate how fun or interesting you are. When you are willing to share your stories, hobbies, and pieces of your life with students, you become interesting to them, and become a person they want to be around. Although you want your content to be contagious, that won't happen unless you've built relationships with your students. That relationship makes you the teacher who they can't wait to see. Once you have that, you will be able to create curiosity and desire when it comes to your content. They'll come to class every day curious to learn more about the subject that fascinates their favorite teacher so much.

Know your target audience.

A successful brand knows its target audience inside out. It meets the needs of the consumers and finds ways to reach them, based on research. As teachers, we have a target audience sitting in front of us every day. When we meet them where they are, we will pique their interest. Find a way to teach your content within the context of their lives, and you'll reach them more easily. Link your lessons to real-world learning and infuse life experiences into instruction to make learning come alive. Research the latest trends and fads, and create lessons around them. Listen to what students talk about in the hallways, in conversations, and in passing, and implement that research into concepts found within your content area. When your students see that what you teach fits into their world, they will become interested in how it can benefit them in the future. If you figure out what drives them, you can personalize content to fit their needs. Relating your material to real-life situations makes it easier for them to understand, learn, and apply it. Attach the subject to their everyday lives, and you will create a brand that they will follow.

Interact with your audience.

The best brands find ways to interact with their audiences. Whether they use social media, advertising, or face-to-face sales, effective brands make people feel as though they are part of something valuable. They demonstrate understanding and express interest in the needs of their customers so that everyone who chooses them feels special. Teachers can do the same by learning alongside students. When your students see that you are willing to be a part of the learning experience with them, they will buy into what you are teaching.

Create assignments and do them with your

students. Sit with them and demonstrate how important your content is to you by modeling your expectations. When you complete an assignment or experiment as well, you show your students that what you are teaching is important. It will become more valuable to them in that moment. It helps bolster your own knowledge, fine-tunes your practice, and puts you in the position of the student. Interacting with your students and content in the moment can level the playing field and show them how much you love what you do.

Make Your Content Contagious by Stepping into Their Shoes

Our students want to know that what they are learning is relevant to them and the world in which they live. They want to know how our lessons will help them in the future, and they want to understand the purpose behind them. If we show them what they're looking for, the content will gain a purpose in their minds. This starts with us and how we teach every day. When we are unmotivated or uninspired, it tells our students that what they are learning is unimportant. When we are excited and enthusiastic about our content, on the other hand, it becomes contagious. If we don't love what we do or the subject we teach, it will come through in our teaching, and our students will react accordingly.

A sure-fire way to make our content relevant to our students is to step into their shoes and teach it as if we were learning it. We often teach the way we enjoy learning, and then assume our students enjoy it as well. Sometimes we put together creative units or spend hours figuring out fun ways to teach a concept, only to find out that our students are less than impressed with our presentation. We then tend to blame them for being unmotivated, and talk about how the fast pace of the world makes it impossible to impress students with presentations that don't include technology or social media. We go from being the biggest fan of our content and exuding enthusiasm to becoming a defender of why our students should love what we teach.

When we have to convince them to enjoy our lessons through an argument, we're failing. They'll never learn to love what we teach if we have to talk them into it. Instead, step into their shoes and figure out what *they* find exciting. Earlier in this book, we delved deeper into how to encourage student ownership, but it is just as important here when we're trying to make our content contagious.

We also need to control our expectations, because they might be setting our students up for failure. Instead of expecting students to learn exactly like we learn, uNforgettable teachers put themselves in their students' shoes and figure out ways to reach them with the lessons they teach. Sometimes that means adjusting our expectations—both for our sakes, and the sakes of our students!

Set Realistic Expectations

Our content can become contagious when we set the right expectations. People enjoy learning what they feel they can master. Even if concepts are difficult, we can be motivated to learn them—*if* we know it's possible. Our content works the same way. When we set expectations within reach of our students, we set them up for success. Once they find success, they will move forward.

Just like with anything else, though, we have to find the right balance for those expectations. Some students will find our content easy, while others will find it difficult. Our goal is to find the perfect balance, to challenge our high achievers, inspire the hard workers, and allow those who struggle to soar. All students can succeed as long as we scaffold our content so it challenges them and stays within reach at the same time.

What we expect of each student will play a big role in whether or not they love what they are learning in class. When we set our expectations too low, we squash the passion for some students, while lowering the standards of others. When we set our expectations too high, we cause some students to give up altogether, while others are made to feel like failures. Instead of one-size-fits-all expectations, we must try to set our goals to meet the specific needs of each student. Our content won't become contagious if we set expectations that students don't feel they can reach. uNforgettable teachers provide realistic expectations for every student, to challenge them to raise their own personal bars and exceed what they set out to achieve. That personalized approach—and the fact that we care enough to take it—will help students fall in love with our content and our brand. Provide a pathway to success that teaches hard work, determination, and grit, and you will become the guide they need to succeed.

Try one of these simple strategies to help set realistic expectations for your students:

- **Survey your students.** Create a short survey that students can take to give you a better understanding of their knowledge of a topic. Include simple questions. Meet with students based on their answers to help determine where they are in regard to understanding. Develop expectations and guidelines that will challenge them based on your findings.

- **Group students based on level.** Some students are more advanced than others, and we have many tools to help us determine where they fall. Group students with others who share the same level of ability. Allow them to create a rubric that will challenge them, and give them ownership over the expectations they need to meet.

- **Create ladder assignments.** A ladder assignment works in a progressive manner. It is one assignment that is split into multiple parts, and the expectations rise as the assignment progresses. For example, if students are writing an essay, break it down into one paragraph at a time and increase expectations with each element. As they move forward in their work, their skills will grow with the increasing expectations. Use the expectation you set for the end of the assignment as the starting point for the next one. As the year continues, students will raise the bar with everything they do, and will become accustomed to exceeding expectations.

Put the right expectations in place and you'll teach students to enjoy the content, and you will consistently challenge them to become better. Put their interests and needs first, and see the content through their eyes, so you can better meet their needs and adapt your expectations. Doing so will lead to better success and enthusiasm in your lessons.

Spread the Good News

When we are excited about something, we talk about it, share it with the world, and get others excited with our enthusiasm. When a toddler takes those first steps, parents share it on social media, make phone calls, and beam with pride. When we accomplish a goal, we share our success and the strategies we used with anyone who will listen. Our passions in life excite us, and we want everyone else to share our excitement with us.

When our students do something amazing, whether in or out of school, they are bursting with excitement. When they achieve something they have worked hard for, a smile stretches across their faces as they make their way up to let us know the good news. We can approach our content in the same way. Although it is tough to be energetic all the time, when we view what we teach as a topic that the world needs to know more about, we will burst at the seams just waiting to share it. When we are just as excited to share what we teach with our students, as we are when we share our passions, our content will become contagious.

Let's create an atmosphere that is filled with excitement about the content we teach. Our students want to see teachers who are happy to be there and who bring a positive spin to every lesson. They want to be taught by teachers who customize expectations to challenge them where they are, so they can rise above and accomplish the impossible. They want to be in classrooms that show how much the teachers love their subject matter. We can spread the good news of our content every day when we bring energy and enthusiasm into our lessons. Our students deserve teachers who are passionate about the knowledge they bestow and the wisdom they provide.

Be uNforgettable by making your content come alive and feel contagious. Whether you build an inspiration wall, adjust your expectations to better suit their needs, or you share your stories of triumph, do what it takes to demonstrate your love for your content, so your students will view it as important and worth pursuing themselves.

uNleash the Love

When we step into the shoes of our students and take a moment to think about the view from where they sit, we can transform their experience. Creating opportunities for them to be the center of attention when it comes to our content will get them excited to share. When we are not afraid to fall in love with what we teach, and share that love of knowledge with our students, we can change how they view what they learn. Teachers who love what they do and are excited about the content they teach will spark curiosity and interest in their students, because teachers who are on fire make learning contagious. How do you achieve this?

- **Reflect.** It can be tough to love everything you teach, and that is OK. Try to find the greatness in it all. When your students see your passion for your content and your love of teaching, they will become curious. They may wonder why you love it so much, or they may just think you are crazy, but you will grab their attention either way. Help to answer that question for them. Show them the reason you love what you do, and uNveil the secret to your craziness. Think about these simple questions as you reflect on how to make your content contagious: What can you do today to make content come alive for every student? What aspects of your content do you love? Is it evident through how you act or teach each day?

- **uNleash.** Be contagious. Sometimes all it takes is a small action to make your content contagious. Highlighting student insight in front of their peers, completing assignments with them, or sharing personal stories about how what you teach has changed your life, can all be impactful. Take action this week. Choose one of the following points that you can uNleash this week, and commit to carrying it out:

- Plan to create an inspiration wall, and involve students in laying it out and deciding what it will focus on.

- Plan an assignment that you will complete with your students during a lesson this week.

- Do something this week that demonstrates your love for what you teach and make it obvious to your students.

- **Get social.** Take a photo of one way you demonstrate love for what you teach. Wear a shirt relating to your content and take a photo, or share an inspiring display your class created. Post it on social media using the hashtag #WeTeachuN, and encourage teachers everywhere!

Define Your Purpose

The two most important days in
your life are the day you were born
and the day you find out why.

—COMMONLY ATTRIBUTED TO MARK TWAIN

Destination Guide Ten

WE CAN CHANGE
LIVES, INSPIRE
STUDENTS, AND
ENCOURAGE
COLLEAGUES WHEN
OUR PERSPECTIVE
IS DRIVEN BY A
SPECIFIC PURPOSE
TO SERVE.

uNveil Your Purpose

YOU WERE BUILT to sail.

A well-built ship that is docked in a harbor is completely safe. The water around it will keep it afloat, and the ropes used to tie it to the dock will keep it from moving. As long as it remains in the harbor, the ship avoids the risk of dangerous waters. The truth, however, is that if a ship remains safely tied to the dock, it will never serve its purpose, because ships weren't built to stay in the harbor. They were built to sail.

As teachers, we often secure ourselves to the safety of docks in the same way, and that may be the very reason we struggle to find our purpose. Although the open sea is scary, taking that leap of faith and venturing out into the vast unknown is the only way we will find what we were made to do. Be brave and untie any ropes that are holding you back, because you were built to sail. Figure out your purpose.

You are uNforgettable.

Your impact is more powerful than you think. You have the opportunity to change the world—but only if you grasp the power of your purpose. You are engaging, creative, innovative, and filled with joy. The energy you exude and the passion you display for those you teach is remarkable.

We can create an impact that lasts a lifetime—but first, we must define our purpose. When we focus on our gifts and share them with those we teach, we can be uNforgettable. Concentrate on spreading your joy, energy, and enthusiasm for teaching to your students and your colleagues. Your students may not remember a specific lesson you taught, a grade they received, or a project you assigned, but they will never forget you. They will remember how you treated them, what you stood for, and how you made them feel every day as they entered your class. When you understand what your students will remember about you, and focus on their perspective, your purpose becomes clear.

German philosopher Friedrich Nietzsche once said, "He who has a why to live can bear almost any how." Knowing your purpose gives you the courage to overcome obstacles, take risks, and face challenges, and your courage will benefit those around you. As a teacher, you will face overwhelming odds, seemingly impossible expectations, and frustrating moments. When these difficult times arise, your students will count on you to remain steadfast. When you understand your purpose, you will have an anchor in those times of trouble, and a guide when you are sailing the open sea.

uNforgettable teachers leave life-altering imprints on their students. You may have an uNforgettable teacher who left that imprint on you, or you may be the teacher that has done it for a student. In order to accomplish such a feat, you must understand exactly what your purpose is, and why it's so important.

Knowing Your Purpose Provides Clarity

In order to be uNforgettable in the classroom, as well as in life, we must have clarity. Clarity is defined in its simplest form as "the state of being clear." We must figure out why we do what we do so that we have clarity, because it will be the rock we stand on during tough times. You might love to teach for many reasons, from wanting to help students become better people to assisting them in their knowledge of concepts. But those are reasons.

Our purpose is different.

To find clarity, we must distinguish between the reasons we love to teach and the purpose that grounds us. If we can't grasp this difference, we'll have trouble overcoming obstacles and frustrations, because we won't understand what our foundation is. Our purpose (our foundation) is to serve our students well. The reasons (our priorities) will all point back to that truth.

Truly uNforgettable teachers know their purpose and their reasons, and have plans for how to achieve them. Your plan for priorities will look simpler and have more to do with lessons, while your plan for purpose includes deeper principles like meeting the needs of students, teaching them life lessons, and being there for them in times of need. Building a plan—and sticking to it—helps you maintain clarity and stay on the path.

Knowing your purpose gives you the ability to clearly see the big picture and focus on what is most important.

Knowing Your Purpose
Provides Perspective

Many of our daily decisions, actions, and choices are based on our perspectives. When we view our teaching through the lens of our purpose to serve students and serve others, our perspective shifts from focusing on our wants first to putting others at the front of the line. We can change lives, inspire students, and encourage colleagues when our perspective is driven by a specific purpose to serve. When we enter our classrooms each day, we make hundreds of decisions. Some of these decisions are small, while others are more intense, but they all make a difference. The actions we take and the choices we make will alter our overall direction in how we teach and how we treat students. These decisions, actions, and choices are often based on our perspectives, and knowing the purpose behind what we do will help us remain grounded in our perspectives.

Our students serve as a perfect gauge to help us determine whether or not we are carrying out our purpose. They are often reflections of the teachers in front of them, and the way they react to situations or behave in our class may be a telling sign of how well we are serving them. When we take a moment to observe them closely, we will be able to determine whether or not we need to move in a different direction, or if we should stay on the same path. They may misbehave, act up, or react in a disrespectful manner from time to time, because they are kids and are human, just like us. But if we are carrying out our purpose successfully and serving our students well, our reactions to their outbursts will be based on love. If we are not, our reactions may be based on an inner desire to take control.

Although there will be times when we become frustrated and overwhelmed, when we understand our purpose we will react negatively less often than we react positively. Sometimes we will be tough and strict, while at other times we will display mercy, but our students should always know what our goals are for them. We must show them that we are there to make sure they become the best persons possible, and that we only want what is best for them. When we pay close attention to those staring back at us each day, we will see our purpose in action. Changing our perspectives to ones that serve others rather than ones that serve ourselves can make all the difference in how we react to our students, and how we handle every situation we come across.

We might not always be able to see the impact we're making, and we might want to give up and head back to the selfish perspective. It is, after all, sometimes easier to deal with students in a quick and harsh manner, instead of in a way that requires time to cultivate results. In the moment it may seem that what we are doing is working, and that may be true, but in the long term, our impact will be more valuable if we take the time to do things right. We must also work to remember those moments, as both examples and pieces of encouragement. uNforgettable teachers keep these moments close by so they can refer to them whenever they begin to doubt.

Digital Moments vs. Printable Moments

We live in a digital culture where we can record life's moments with the devices in our pockets. Our phones might be chock-full of pictures and videos we've probably forgotten about. In our teaching lives, we have digital moments that we record every day as well. They are important memories we cherish, laugh about, and hold dear, but they don't define our purpose. They may be memories of when colleagues complimented us or when the commute to work was traffic-free, and they are all amazing experiences that impact us and bring smiles to our faces. In reality, though, they are short-term memories that fade as time passes.

TEACHERS HAVE MANY PRINTABLE MOMENTS. WHETHER STUDENTS COME BACK TO VISIT, WRITE A LETTER, OR HUG YOU FOR NO APPARENT REASON, THEY ARE DEMONSTRATING YOUR IMPACT.

Printable moments, on the other hand, are the pictures we print and frame to display around our homes. They remind us of what is important and who we are at our core. They are the moments that transform us, the ones we wait for, the ones worth saving. We have the same types of moments as teachers. When students make a specific effort to show their appreciation for what we have done for them, they give us a printable moment. When they grasp a concept that we made sure they did not give up on, they give us a printable moment. These are the moments that display the outcomes of our purpose. Ultimately, we serve others so they can become better, and we don't expect anything in return. But when we commit to carrying out this purpose, we find rewards. It may take days, weeks, or even years to come into view, but sometimes the greatest things in life are worth waiting for, and these are the ones that remind us that we are uNforgettable. Some examples of printable moments in a teacher's life are:

- When students you taught many years ago come back to visit just to say thank you for the impact you had on them.

- When students show you the home screen on their phone, and you are part of the picture collage in the display.

- When the most difficult students in the class, the ones who drive you crazy, demonstrate how much they really need you.

- When students accidentally call you Mom or Dad.

Teachers have many printable moments. Whether students come back to visit, write a letter, or hug you for no apparent reason, they are demonstrating your impact. Don't take these moments for granted; cherish them. These are the moments that show you how you're impacting others. These moments show that you are changing the world, and they are the ones that reveal your purpose. When you compile your printable moments in teaching, it will transform your perspective and confirm your purpose.

uNravel a Plan to Focus and Fine-Tune Your Purpose

Look toward the horizon.

If you have been seasick, then you know it is one of the worst experiences to go through. Between the dizziness and nausea that course through your body with every passing wave, you feel like you just want to pass out. The reason most people get seasick, however, is because they focus completely on what is directly below them. As they watch the waves on the side of the boat, concentrating on the ups and downs, the smells of the sea, and the movement of the boat, they lose their sense of equilibrium. They lose sight of everything around them, and rather than enjoying the ride, find themselves wishing they were never there in the first place.

The secret to maintaining your balance and your stomach in these situations is to focus on the horizon rather than the waves. When we take the time to look ahead at the fixed landscape, we avoid falling prey to the crashing waves that try to bring us down.

As teachers, we may sometimes lose our long view and start to question our purpose. We may face overwhelming situations that make us feel like we are stuck in a never-ending cycle. During these times, we must focus on the fact that our purpose is bigger than the waves trying to bring us down. When we concentrate on the horizon in front of us, rather than the waves beneath us, we find the strength to carry out our purpose.

You'll be faced with times when you don't feel you can achieve the expectations others have set for you, and get angry about the gossip being spread throughout the building. Set your eyes on the students first, and remember what your purpose is, and you'll find your feet again. Although we may still feel a bit queasy from time to time due to the waves crashing into us, focusing on the horizon will give us balance and help us recover.

Use two simple strategies to define, remember, and continue your purpose: the Write It, Read It Strategy and the Purpose Statement. When you incorporate these into your daily plans, your sense of purpose will grow stronger every day, and you'll find it easier to navigate those waves.

The Write It, Read It Strategy

This strategy provides a simple way to revisit your purpose and evaluate how well you are carrying it out. This two-day process brings structure and routine into your day and helps you focus solely on reflection. The way it works is simple: Set aside a few minutes to write down your thoughts on one day, and then set a separate amount of time the next day to revisit those thoughts and read them with an eye to taking action. When we keep journals, we often write a lot, but we never go back and revisit our thoughts. The key here is the revisiting step, because it encourages action and improvement.

Implement this strategy and you will start to reflect on the things that happen, and build ways to fix them.

The Write It portion of this strategy takes advantage of the power of the written word. Studies have shown that when we write things down we are far better at remembering them. The same concept works when it comes to developing and understanding your purpose. Follow these simple steps each day to help maintain your purpose and become better through reflection:

Step One: Choose an amount of time (between five and ten minutes) that you will use to reflect, and add it to your daily schedule or calendar. The goal is to write down your reflections and key moments while they are fresh in your mind. You will meditate on them later during the Read It portion of the strategy.

Step Two: Choose one to three key moments from your day that you want to reflect on, and list them. Limiting your moments to three will force you to choose only the most impactful and memorable moments. This will help you eliminate the digital moments that do not impact your purpose.

Step Three: Write three specific sentences after each key moment. Limiting your explanations means you will be able to reflect in a short amount of time.

- Sentence One: Focus on why this moment had an impact on you or how it impacted someone else.

- Sentence Two: Write down how this moment is related to your purpose of serving others.

- Sentence Three: Write down your thoughts on how this moment will help you improve as a teacher and as a person.

Every teacher has a busy schedule and often juggles many responsibilities on any given day. Make this short routine part of your day, though, and you'll reap the benefits. Build it into your schedule as an appointment that you never miss. Over time, you will find that the habit of writing down moments that define your day helps you fine-tune your purpose.

The Read It portion means taking the time to read what you have written down during your reflection. In order to fully reflect on where you are on the path to your purpose, you must make time to read what you have written. Follow these simple steps each day to help maintain your purpose and become better through reflection:

Step One: Choose an amount of time (between five and ten minutes) that you will use to read and reflect, and add it to your daily schedule or calendar. Do this the day after you have written your reflection points in the Write It portion of the strategy.

Step Two: Read through your key points and choose one that you will take action on. Starting with one key moment allows you to go even deeper into it than if you were to try to take on all three.

Step Three: Read the three sentences you have written beside the moment you chose. Find a way to take action during the day based on what you have read. If the moment is about how someone impacted you in a positive way, try to do the same for someone else. If it is something negative, do your best to reverse it into a positive occurrence during the day. The key is to take what you read and do something with it that will help you fulfill your purpose of serving others.

When you are going through the Read It portion of this strategy, let things sink in, and use the words you have formulated to guide you each day. Once you begin the habit of writing down moments and reading them after they have occurred, you will find that you naturally do it every day. This practice will change your perspective, and help you look at the bigger picture more often.

Create a Purpose Statement

Once you have taken the time to start observing the bigger picture, move forward and develop a purpose statement. This can be anything from a simple sentence to a paragraph explaining your purpose, but it must be designed for you and by you. When our purpose is to serve our students and others, and that is our foundation, the purpose statement may be very specific: "I will serve my students by committing to offer them a voice and input into their learning." This statement will remind you to focus on students when you're in the classroom. A purpose statement might also be: "I will serve my students by getting to know their personal stories and implementing their interests into my teaching." This statement reminds you to build relationships and rely on them during the toughest days.

Your purpose statement may change slightly over time, but the foundation should always be the same. Your ultimate goal is to serve those around you, whether it is your students or your colleagues. This is a crucial step in carrying out your purpose on a daily basis—but the process might change. Use your reflections to determine whether your purpose statement is still serving your foundation or not, and adjust it as necessary to accomplish your goals.

Create a purpose statement based on your passions, daily observations, and reflections. Place that statement on a sticky note and put it where you will see it regularly. Leave it in multiple places, where you know you will find it throughout your daily routine. When times are great, this sticky note will make you smile. When times are tough, it will help you see the light at the end of the tunnel. Sometimes the simplest action is what we need to encourage us as we move forward.

To be uNforgettable to your students, remind yourself often of your purpose. Take the time to create your purpose statement to teach yourself more about what you believe, and to give yourself something to lean on when you come across frustrations. uNravel your purpose through observation, reflection, and a daily reminder, and you will see your impact flourish and come alive.

uNleash Your Memories

Your purpose is powerful. Those you teach are counting on you to have their best interests at heart. What you believe to be your purpose can have a direct effect on those in front of you each day. Set your foundation and base your lessons and interactions around those you serve. Remember why you do what you do each day and never forget the lasting impact you have as a teacher.

- **Reflect.** Sometimes our purpose can become clouded because we concern ourselves with everything else going on around us. How can you make your purpose the foundation of what you do each day? How does your purpose affect what you do each day? Think about those you serve. If you aren't concentrating on your purpose first, how well are you truly carrying it out?

- **uNleash.** Our memories are powerful reminders of our purpose. You can uNleash inspiration for yourself by taking on these two action steps today:
  - Create your Purpose Statement and write it down on a sticky note. Place the note where it is visible to you each day. Read it every morning before you begin teaching and rely on it to drive your teaching forward.
  - Write down one to three impactful memories that remind you of WHY you teach. Read them each day this week. Practice this process bi-weekly or once a month to remind you of your impact.

- **Get social.** Take a picture of your Purpose Statement and share it to inspire others. Post your picture on social media using the hashtag #WeTeachuN.

Don't Quit

It always seems impossible until it's done. — COMMONLY ATTRIBUTED TO NELSON MANDELA

Destination Guide
Final Thoughts

EVERY STUDENT
YOU COME INTO
CONTACT WITH HAS
A STORY THAT IS
YET TO BE TOLD.

uNveil Your Resilience

UNFORGETTABLE TEACHERS ARE the Navy Seals of teaching.

Navy Seal training is arguably some of the most grueling in the world. The training includes Hell Week, when Navy Seals will spend nearly six days of intense training going through a series of tests that measure physical endurance, mental toughness, teamwork, and the ability to perform under pressure on no more than four hours of sleep for the whole week. Two hundred and twenty will volunteer, but on average only twenty will pass without quitting.

A single bell, visible throughout the training, is the one thing that can set them free. All a soldier needs to do to get a warm meal and a good night's sleep is to ring the bell and quit. They are constantly being told that they aren't good enough or strong enough, and don't have what it takes to be a Navy Seal, and the vast majority eventually give in to the physical and mental stress and give up. The soldiers who make it, however, though they are not necessarily the strongest or the smartest, have a desire, above all else, to be a Seal.

As uNforgettable teachers, we are the Navy Seals in education, and we exist for our students. We understand that the kids we teach are counting on us to refuse to ring the bell and give up on them. When the pressure seems too great and the frustrations pile up, we don't quit, but rather push forward with passion and focus. Remember that it is not necessarily the smartest or most creative teachers who become uNforgettable, but those who have the desire, above all else, to influence, empower, and change the lives of their students for the better.

You are powerful.

Every student you come into contact with has a story that is yet to be told. Many of them stand at a fork in the road, looking to you to tell them which way to go. You have the power to either steer them down a path that leads to success ... or down one that will lead them astray. If you've built relationships with them and shown that you care for them, they'll trust you to guide them. If you haven't, and they're still filled with anxiety in your presence, they'll turn away and make their own decisions. uNforgettable teachers hold power in their hands.

You have been gifted with unimaginable responsibility: the ability to influence the future, to mold minds, to impact destinies, and to change lives. In order to handle such power, take a look at the bigger picture. Teaching is about those you serve every day, and when you put the needs of your students first, and use your abilities to better the world by wielding your positive power, you impact reality in memorable ways. The most memorable teachers are those who bring what only they can bring to the classroom: themselves. You become uNforgettable when you are willing to be yourself with your students, and refuse to give up on them by ringing that bell.

You hold the power of influence in your hands, so use it well.

uNravel the Principles of a Navy Seal

Navy Seals are an elite military force of leaders, team-mates, and visionaries. They take on the most difficult missions and carry them out with excellence. To be part of a Navy Seal team is to be a member of a family that has laughed together, cried together, and battled together. The bond between them is unbreakable, and the reason for their long-term success only begins with training. The true strength that helps them carry out mission after mission lies in the principles that they live by each day.

uNforgettable teachers are also leaders, teammates, and visionaries. There is nothing quite like the unspoken bond shared by teachers. We are in this together, and ultimately we understand that our mission is to work with one another to change the lives of those we teach. Sometimes all we need is a little encouragement to get us through the day. Other times, we may need a helping hand or a shoulder to cry on to help us continue moving forward. In either situation, we will be better together than we ever could have been alone. To teach like a Navy Seal is to be part of a family, and to live by a set of principles that allows us to succeed no matter what is thrown our way. Anytime you feel frustrated, overwhelmed, or as though you are ready to ring the bell, remember to teach like a Seal. Follow these seven Navy Seal principles to remind you that you are uNforgettable, and together #WeTeachuN.

Principle One: Humility Is a True Sign of Strength

Navy Seals do not seek credit, but rather live to serve. They accomplish what some deem impossible because they are willing to accept responsibility for their actions, rely on others when they do not have all the answers, and work together for the greater good.

uNforgettable teachers are humble and possess servant hearts. That humility allows them to genuinely make others better and change the lives of the students they teach. When we live by this principle and practice humility, we demonstrate strength. The strongest teachers act in selfless love for those who may never be able to repay them. Harness your humility and let your passion for teaching help you work with others to accomplish the unimaginable.

Principle Two: The Little Things Can Make a Lasting Impact

Navy Seal commander Admiral William McRaven gave a speech in Texas where he focused on his famous first commandment: "Make your bed in the morning." His purpose was to demonstrate the power of the little things in life. When we complete this simple task before doing anything else, it encourages us to continue to complete tasks as the day moves forward. By the end of the day, we will have accomplished many things, all because we began by successfully accomplishing one simple thing.

uNforgettable teachers face hurdles almost daily, which

keep them on the edge of their seats. Focus on the small successes that you have each day, and you can overcome the obstacles that try to block your progress. When we pay attention to the little things that matter to our students, we will be able to impact them on a grand scale. Start each day with a commitment to embrace the little things you face and the small successes you see in your teaching. They will strengthen you and lead you on your journey to make a lasting impact.

Principle Three: Positive Influences Help Us Flourish

A Navy Seal, on any given day, can be surrounded by three impactful people: a superior (who is above them in rank), their peers (who are by their sides), and the new recruits (who stand where they once stood). Any of these people might be mentors to push the Seal to continually learn and improve.

uNforgettable teachers are also surrounded by influencers every day. Some tend to sway toward the negative, some pull toward the positive, and some remain neutral. To be the best you can be, surround yourself with positive influences, much like the Navy Seals do:

- Find others who have more experience than you and who you respect, and learn from them.

- Find others who you consider as peers that you admire, and allow them to push your boundaries.

- Find others who are where you once were and are remarkable, and collaborate with them.

When we surround ourselves with positive influences at every stage of teaching, we learn more than we ever thought possible, give more than we ever did before, and grow in ways that we never knew we could.

Principle Four: Critics Are Crucial for Success

During Hell Week, Navy Seals are bombarded by critics intent on tearing them down. Everywhere they look, there are people reminding them that they don't have what it takes to be a Seal, and they are pushed to the brink of exhaustion to make them quit. These critics, however, bring out the inner strength and drive that a soldier must show to make it to the next level. Without these critics, they would not be able to succeed.

uNforgettable teachers are thankful for the critics. We need those who will challenge our thinking, help us learn the power of discernment, and give us an opportunity to grow. They teach us what it means to push boundaries, and can lead us to the verge of innovation. Critics do not bother with those who remain the same year after year. Instead, critics focus on innovative thinkers who embrace new ideas, because they are the ones who ultimately rise above and raise the bar. When we embrace this principle, our outlook changes, and we are able to find the inner strength we need to succeed during even the toughest of days.

Principle Five: Giving More Than
Expected Helps Us Rise

Those who make it to the end of Seal training give more than they ever thought they could. To make it through the pressure put on them, Navy Seals must rely on one another to get them through. When they are on the brink of exhaustion and feel as though they are about to fail, they rely on each other for encouragement. One would expect the opposite, but Navy Seals are not competing with their fellow soldiers. Instead, they want them to succeed. They will often give more of themselves, just to help the person standing next to them to stay strong.

uNforgettable teachers do more than expected. They embrace student questioning, enhance learning, and inspire students every day. When students offer ideas to make learning better, the teachers give them the opportunity to carry out the ideas. Teachers who exceed the expectations of their students will provide an environment where the ones doing the learning are the ones with the loudest voices. They will create an atmosphere of trust and vulnerability in order to help students succeed and thrive. Our students need teachers who give them more than they ask for, in order to accomplish more than they ever thought they could. Living out this principle helps us to rise above the status quo and gives our students the opportunity to follow our lead and do the same.

Principle Six: Wisdom Is Gained Through Failure

No Navy Seal can make it through training without failure. Some will physically fail along the way, while others fail mentally, but those who succeed are the ones who learn from their failures and push forward, rather than giving into them and giving up. With each mistake they make, they become stronger and wiser, and that leads them to the finish line.

uNforgettable teachers gain wisdom through failure. We acquire wisdom over time, often through the tough experiences we have in life. Such wisdom is an invaluable asset that all teachers should strive to obtain. If you have the willpower to get up every time you fall, then you will grow. You will be able to set the example for the students you lead, and you will understand their frustrations. You will have the chance to help guide your peers because you will have earned their respect. Every mistake gives you a chance to learn, and the chance to collect more wisdom.

ALTHOUGH CONTENT AND CURRICULUM ARE NECESSARY FOR A WELL-ROUNDED EDUCATION, LOVE IS WHAT TRULY TRANSFORMS STUDENTS' LIVES.

Principle Seven: A Student Who Is Loved Can Learn

Soldiers become a family as they become Navy Seals. They grow to genuinely love one another and become willing to put their lives on the line for those who stand by their side. No matter what the circumstances, they are able to overcome them because the love they have for their team is greater than the obstacles placed in front of them.

uNforgettable teachers know that love is important. Although content and curriculum are necessary for a well-rounded education, love is what truly transforms students' lives. The smiles on their faces at the end of the day matter more than the grades on their report cards. When we approach our students with a heart that cares, and treat them like family, they begin to believe that they can overcome any obstacle, conquer any fear, and learn any lesson—all because someone in their life showed them that they matter. Living by this principle and demonstrating its truth can make all the difference in the lives of those we teach.

uNleash the Future

We can make a greater impact when we share our genius. uNforgettable teachers take what we have learned and inspire others by passing it on.

- **Reflect.** How can you inspire fellow teachers to be uNforgettable? What can you do to set the example for those around you?

- **uNleash.** Pass it on by choosing one of the following options to complete this week:

  - Share this book with a colleague who you think is uNforgettable, or who you feel can benefit from the content inside.

  - Pass on a word of encouragement to a fellow teacher who inspires you.

- **Get social.** Use the sentence frame "An uNforgettable teacher is _____" and fill in the blank. Be creative, and post it on social media using the hashtag #WeTeachuN.

Meet the Author

Chuck Poole is a veteran teacher who has made it his mission to inspire and encourage teachers all over the world to be the best they can be. He is the visionary behind Teachonomy.com, and the host of the *Teachonomy Talks* podcast. Chuck is the producer of the uNseries for Times 10 Books, and the author of *uNforgettable: Your Roadmap to Being the Teacher They Never Forget*, the first book in the series. Chuck lives in New Jersey with his wife, Amanda, and enjoys mentoring, creating laughter in the classroom, and the continued pursuit of his next adventure. Follow Chuck on Twitter @cpoole27.

MORE FROM

The uN series

The uNseries: Teaching Reimagined

The uNseries is for teachers who love the uNlovable, accept the uNacceptable, rebuild the broken, and help the genius soar. Through each book in The uNseries, you will learn how to continue your growth as a teacher, leader, and influencer. The goal is that together we can become better than we ever could be alone. Each chapter uNveils an important principle to ponder, uNravels a plan that you can put into place to make an even greater impact, and uNleashes an action step for you to take to be a better educator. Learn more about **The uNseries and everything uN** at unseries.com.

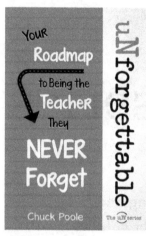

uNforgettable
Your Roadmap to Being the Teacher They Never Forget
by Chuck Poole (@cpoole27)

These 10 destinations will give you the inspiration and knowledge you need to take action and leave a lasting impression for years to come. Chuck Poole will be your guide. Through every twist and turn, you will be empowered, encouraged, and equipped to reimagine teaching in a way that will influence your students for a lifetime.

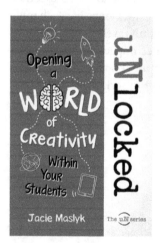

uNlocked:
Opening a World of Creativity Within Your Students
By Jacie Maslyk (@DrJacieMaslyk)

Creativity flows within us all. It allows teachers to reignite a passion for learning and offers students an outlet that can lead to endless possibilities. Creativity is essential, and Jacie Maslyk helps you and your students uNleash its full potential with her new book, *uNlocked: Opening a World of Creativity Within Your Students.*

In this second book in The uNseries, you will learn how to **uNlock creativity in powerful ways** to help you create undeniable learning experiences for your students, and you will discover the keys you need to uNlock your students' full potential for creativity.

TIMES 10 BOOKS

HACKING EDUCATION
10 Quick Fixes For Every School

By Mark Barnes (@markbarnes19) & Jennifer Gonzalez (@cultofpedagogy)

In the award-winning first Hack Learning Series book, *Hacking Education*, Mark Barnes and Jennifer Gonzalez employ decades of teaching experience and hundreds of discussions with education thought leaders to show you how to find and hone the quick fixes that every school and classroom need. Using a Hacker's mentality, they provide **one Aha moment after another** with 10 Quick Fixes For Every School—solutions to everyday problems and teaching methods that any teacher or administrator can implement immediately.

"Barnes and Gonzalez don't just solve problems; they turn teachers into hackers—a transformation that is right on time."

—DON WETTRICK, AUTHOR OF *PURE GENIUS*

HACKING PROJECT BASED LEARNING
10 Easy Steps to PBL and Inquiry in the Classroom
By Ross Cooper (@rosscoops31) and Erin Murphy (@murphysmusings5)

As questions and mysteries around PBL and inquiry continue to swirl, experienced classroom teachers and school administrators Ross Cooper and Erin Murphy have written a book that will empower those intimidated by PBL to cry, "I can do this!" while at the same time providing added value for those who are already familiar with the process. Impacting teachers and leaders around the world, *Hacking Project Based Learning* demystifies what PBL is all about with **10 hacks that construct a simple path** that educators and students can easily follow to achieve success. Forget your prior struggles with project based learning. This book makes PBL an amazing gift you can give all students tomorrow!

"Hacking Project Based Learning is a classroom essential. Its ten simple 'hacks' will guide you through the process of setting up a learning environment in which students will thrive from start to finish."

—DANIEL H. PINK, *NEW YORK TIMES* BESTSELLING AUTHOR OF *DRIVE*

HACKING ASSESSMENT

10 Ways To Go Gradeless In a Traditional Grades School

By Starr Sackstein (@mssackstein)

In the bestselling *Hacking Assessment,* award-winning teacher and world-renowned formative assessment expert Starr Sackstein unravels one of education's oldest mysteries: How to assess learning without grades—even in a school that uses numbers, letters, GPAs, and report cards. While many educators can only muse about the possibility of a world without grades, teachers like Sackstein are **reimagining education**. In this unique, eagerly-anticipated book, Sackstein shows you exactly how to create a remarkable no-grades classroom like hers, a vibrant place where students grow, share, thrive, and become independent learners who never ask, "What's this worth?"

"The beauty of the book is that it is not an empty argument against grades—but rather filled with valuable alternatives that are practical and will help to refocus the classroom on what matters most."

—ADAM BELLOW, WHITE HOUSE PRESIDENTIAL INNOVATION FELLOW

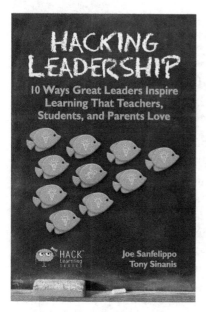

HACKING LEADERSHIP
10 Ways Great Leaders Inspire Learning That Teachers, Students, and Parents Love

By Joe Sanfelippo (@joe_sanfelippo) and Tony Sinanis (@tonysinanis)

In the runaway bestseller *Hacking Leadership*, internationally known school leaders Joe Sanfelippo and Tony Sinanis bring readers inside schools that few stakeholders have ever seen—places where students not only come first but have a unique voice in teaching and learning. Sanfelippo and Sinanis ignore the bureaucracy that stifles many leaders, focusing instead on building a culture of **engagement, transparency and, most important, fun.** *Hacking Leadership* has superintendents, principals, and teacher leaders around the world employing strategies they never before believed possible and learning how to lead from the middle. Want to revolutionize teaching and learning at your school or district? *Hacking Leadership* is your blueprint. Read it today, energize teachers and learners tomorrow!

"The authors do a beautiful job of helping leaders focus inward, instead of outward. This is an essential read for leaders who are, or want to lead, learner-centered schools."

—GEORGE COUROS, AUTHOR OF *THE INNOVATOR'S MINDSET*

HACKING SCHOOL CULTURE
Designing Compassionate Classrooms
By Angela Stockman (@angelastockman) and Ellen Feig Gray (@ellenfeiggray)

Bullying prevention and character-building programs are deepening our awareness of how today's kids struggle and how we might help, but many agree: They aren't enough to create school cultures where students and staff flourish. This inspired Angela Stockman and Ellen Feig Gray to begin seeking out systems and educators who were getting things right. Their experiences taught them that the real game changers are using a human-centered approach. Inspired by other design thinkers, many teachers are creating learning environments where seeking a greater understanding of themselves and others is the highest standard. They're also realizing that compassion is best cultivated in the classroom, not the boardroom or the auditorium. It's here that we learn how to pull one another close. It's here that we begin to negotiate the distances between us, too.

"*Hacking School Culture: Designing Compassionate Classrooms* is a valuable addition to the Hack Learning Series. It provides concrete support and suggestions for teachers to improve their interactions with their students at the same time they enrich their own professional experiences. Although primarily aimed at K–12 classrooms, the authors' insightful suggestions have given me, a veteran college professor, new insights into positive classroom dynamics which I have already begun to incorporate into my classes."

—LOUISE HAINLINE, PH.D., PROFESSOR OF PSYCHOLOGY, BROOKLYN COLLEGE OF CUNY

HACKING EARLY LEARNING
10 Building Blocks to Success in Pre-K–3 That All Teachers and School Leaders Should Know

By Jessica Cabeen (@jessicacabeen)

School readiness, closing achievement gaps, partnering with families, and innovative learning are just a few of the reasons the early learning years are the most critical years in a child's life. In what ways have schools lost the critical components of early learning—preschool through third grade—and how can we intentionally bring those ideas and instructional strategies back? In *Hacking Early Learning*, kindergarten school leader, early childhood education specialist, and Minnesota State Principal of the Year Jessica Cabeen provides strategies for teachers, principals, and district administrators for best practices in preschool through third grade, including connecting these strategies to all grade levels.

"Jessica Cabeen is not afraid to say she's learned from her mistakes and misconceptions. But it is those mistakes and misconceptions that qualify her to write this book, with its wonderfully user-friendly format. For each problem specified, there is a hack and actionable advice presented as "What You Can Do Tomorrow" and "A Blueprint for Full Implementation." Jessica's leadership is informed by both head and heart and, because of that, her wisdom will be of value to those who wish to teach and lead in the early childhood field."

—RAE PICA, EARLY CHILDHOOD EDUCATION KEYNOTE SPEAKER
AND AUTHOR OF *WHAT IF EVERYBODY UNDERSTOOD CHILD
DEVELOPMENT?*

Adam Chamberlin & Svetoslav Matejic

QUIT POINT

UNDERSTANDING APATHY,
ENGAGEMENT, AND MOTIVATION
IN THE CLASSROOM

QUIT POINT:
Understanding Apathy, Engagement, and Motivation in the Classroom

By Adam Chamberlin and Svetoslav Matejic (@pomme_ed)

Two classroom teachers grew tired of apathy in their classrooms, so they asked two simple but crucial questions: Why do students quit? And more important, what should we do about it? In *Quit Point: Understanding Apathy, Engagement, and Motivation in the Classroom*, authors Chamberlin and Matejic present a new way of approaching those issues. The Quit Point—their theory on how, why, and when people quit and how to stop quitting before it happens—will **transform how teachers reach the potential of each and every student.**

Quit Point reveals how to confront apathy and build student engagement; interventions to challenge students to keep going; and how to experience a happier, more fulfilling, teaching experience—starting tomorrow. Researchers, school leaders, and teachers have wondered for centuries what makes students stop working. Now, the answer is finally here. Read *Quit Point* today and stop quitting in your school or class before it begins.

HACKING ENGAGEMENT
50 Tips & Tools to Engage Teachers and Learners Daily
By James Alan Sturtevant (@jamessturtevant)

Some students hate your class. Others are just bored. Many are too nice, or too afraid, to say anything about it. Don't let it bother you; it happens to the best of us. But now, it's **time to engage!** In *Hacking Engagement*, the seventh book in the Hack Learning Series, veteran high school teacher, author, and popular podcaster James Sturtevant provides 50—that's right five-oh—tips and tools that will engage even the most reluctant learners daily. Sold in dozens of countries around the world, *Hacking Engagement* has become an educator's go-to guide for better student engagement in all grades and subjects. In fact, this book is so popular, Sturtevant penned a follow-up, *Hacking Engagement Again*, which brings 50 more powerful strategies. Find both at HackLearningBooks.com.

HACKING DIGITAL LEARNING STRATEGIES
10 Ways to Launch EdTech Missions in Your Classroom

By Shelly Sanchez Terrell (@ShellTerrell)

In this breakthrough book, international EdTech presenter and NAPW Woman of the Year Shelly Sanchez Terrell demonstrates the power of EdTech Missions—lessons and projects that inspire learners to use web tools and social media to innovate, research, collaborate, problem-solve, campaign, crowd fund, crowdsource, and publish. The 10 Missions in *Hacking DLS* are more than enough to transform how teachers integrate technology, but there's also much more here. Included in the book is a **38-page Mission Toolkit**, complete with reproducible mission cards, badges, polls, and other handouts that you can copy and distribute to students immediately.

"The secret to Shelly's success as an education collaborator on a global scale is that she shares information most revered by all educators, information that is original, relevant, and vetted, combining technology with proven education methodology in the classroom. This book provides relevance to a 21st-century educator."

—THOMAS WHITBY, AUTHOR, PODCASTER, BLOGGER, CONSULTANT, CO-FOUNDER OF #EDCHAT

HACKING CLASSROOM MANAGEMENT
10 Ideas To Help You Become the Type of Teacher They Make Movies About

By Mike Roberts (@baldroberts)

Utah English Teacher of the Year and sought-after speaker Mike Roberts brings you 10 quick and easy classroom management hacks that will **make your classroom the place to be** for all your students. He shows you how to create an amazing learning environment that actually makes discipline, rules, and consequences obsolete, no matter if you're a new teacher or a 30-year veteran teacher.

"Mike writes from experience; he's learned, sometimes the hard way, what works and what doesn't, and he shares those lessons in this fine little book. The book is loaded with specific, easy-to-apply suggestions that will help any teacher create and maintain a classroom where students treat one another with respect, and where they learn."
—CHRIS CROWE, ENGLISH PROFESSOR AT BYU, PAST PRESIDENT OF ALAN, AUTHOR OF *DEATH COMING UP THE HILL*, *GETTING AWAY WITH MURDER: THE TRUE STORY OF THE EMMETT TILL CASE*; *MISSISSIPPI TRIAL, 1955*

HACKING THE WRITING WORKSHOP
Redesign with Making in Mind

*By Angela Stockman
(@AngelaStockman)*

Agility matters. This is what Angela Stockman learned when she left the classroom over a decade ago to begin supporting young writers and their teachers in schools. What she learned transformed her practice and led to the publication of her primer on this topic: *Make Writing: 5 Teaching Strategies that Turn Writer's Workshop Into a Maker Space.* Now, Angela is back with more stories from the road and **plenty of new thinking to share.** In *Make Writing*, Stockman upended the traditional writing workshop by combining it with the popular ideas that drive the maker space. Now, she is expanding her concepts and strategies and breaking new ground in *Hacking the Writing Workshop.*

"Good writing is good thinking. This is a book about how to think better, for yourself and with others."

—DAVE GRAY, FOUNDER OF XPLANE, AND AUTHOR OF *THE CONNECTED COMPANY, GAMESTORMING,* AND *LIMINAL THINKING*

RESOURCES FROM TIMES 10

SITES:
times10books.com
hacklearning.org
hacklearningbooks.com
unseries.com
teachonomy.com

PODCASTS:
hacklearningpodcast.com
jamesalansturtevant.com/podcast
teachonomy.com/podcast

FREE TOOLKIT FOR TEACHERS:
hacklearningtoolkit.com

ON TWITTER:
@HackMyLearning
#HackLearning
#HackLearningDaily
#WeTeachuN
#HackingLeadership
#HackingMath
#HackingLiteracy
#HackingEngagement
#HackingHomework

#HackingPBL
#MakeWriting
#EdTechMissions
#MovieTeacher
#HackingEarlyLearning
#CompassionateClassrooms
#HackGoogleEdu
#ParentMantras
#QuitPoint

HACK LEARNING ON FACEBOOK:
facebook.com/hacklearningseries

HACK LEARNING ON INSTAGRAM:
hackmylearning

X10

Vision, Experience, Action

Times 10 is helping all education stakeholders improve every aspect of teaching and learning. We are committed to solving big problems with simple ideas. We bring you content from experts, shared through multiple channels, including books, podcasts, and an array of social networks. Our mantra is simple: Read it today; fix it tomorrow. Stay in touch with us at Times10Books.com, at #HackLearning on Twitter, and on the Hack Learning Facebook page.